www.iamsuccess.net

BUSINESS 101

*Create Your Own Business
in One Day*

2008 Edition
IamSuccess Books
Copyright © 2008 by IamSuccess LLC
ISBN: 1440432635
EAN-13: 9781440432637
Written By: J. Success
Cover Design: www.sohocreative.com

Table Of Contents

Introduction **5**

Part I: Developing the Mind **6**
What is Entrepreneurship 7
Mindset of an Entrepreneur 8
Qualities of Successful People 9
Networking 12

Part II: Business Planning **16**
Business Concept Model 17
Features vs. Benefits 19
Vision and Mission Statements 20
Opportunity Recognition 21
Marketing 24
Business Structures 34
Benefits of each Business Structure 39
Financial Data 40
Financing 44
Copyright 49

Part III: Business Plan Template **52**
Executive Summary 53
Business Concept 54
Business Organization 59
Marketing Plan 62
Financial Plan 65
Conclusion 69
Glossary 70

This book is dedicated to my friend Nick Hale who one day in 2002 just up and said to me, why don't you start a business. It had never dawned on me before that moment, that I was capable of owning my own business. Everyday since then, nothing is impossible

Introduction

This workshop and workbook was created by J. Success in the summer of 2004. After setting up and teaching numerous entrepreneurship programs with other curriculums, I felt that it would benefit students most if I could teach all the topics in one day. If a student can learn everything in one sitting and have the workbook to use as a reference, then they would be able to start their own companies faster and therefore not have to wait to pursue their dreams. Patience is a virtue but when you are focused on a dream, nothing should stand in your way, especially not a 12-week class that can be taught in one day.

Entrepreneur programs are essential in today's world with the occurrences of "downsizing" becoming so common. We do not want to become dependant upon a job when the term "job security" has become a thing of the past. With entrepreneurs being essential in the development and economy of communities, we want to educate people on how to develop their own companies, become leaders, as well as create jobs for others.

This workbook was developed in order to teach students the basics that are required to start their own company. It is an intense workshop that touches on all the necessities that shape the modern entrepreneur.   This workbook compliments a workshop that was created for **_convenience_**, without sacrificing **_content_**. Many entrepreneurship programs feel that it takes a vast amount of time to teach the skills that are required to start your own company but we feel that it's not how much you teach, but what you teach. **_Quality over Quantity_** is the key to this workshop and workbook. This workshop is developed for students that have an incredible desire to change their lives and start their own companies, therefore they will soak up the information that we provide.

The first thing you need to do is decide on the goals for your business. What do you personally want to get out of it? How many hours do you want to work? How many employees do you want to have? How much money do you want to make? The idea here is to get as clear a vision as possible of what your business will look like when it is established so you'll know what needs to be done to get there.

Part I
Developing the Mind

If I believe that I can be successful, then I will be...the hardest part is believing it can happen to me.

- J. Success -

What is Entrepreneurship

Qualities of an entrepreneur

1. _____
2. _____
3. _____
4. _____
5. _____
6. _____
7. _____
8. _____
9. _____
10. _____
11. _____
12. _____
13. _____
14. _____
15. _____
16. _____
17. _____
18. _____
19. _____
20. _____

Definitions:

Entrepreneur – A person who organizes, operates and assumes the risk for a business venture

Entrepreneurship - The organization, management, and assumption of risks of a business or enterprise, usually implying an element of change or challenge and a new opportunity

Five Qualities that J. Success feels entrepreneurs should have:

1. Self Educators
2. Faithful
3. Diligent/Thorough
4. Motivated
5. Patient

"Take Small Steps Towards Your Goal Each Day"

To Do List

1. _____
2. _____
3. _____
4. _____
5. _____

Why is Entrepreneurship good for me?

_____

_____

_____

_____

_____

Motivational Topics
The Mindset of an Entrepreneur

1. **Attitude Is Everything** - (Success Is A State Of Mind)
2. **You Control Your Destiny** - (Successful People Control Their Destinies)
3. **Develop A "Whatever It Takes" Attitude** – (To have what you've never had you must do what you've never done)
4. **Develop A Plan And Write It Down** - (You Have To Know Where You Are Going)
5. **Self Development** - (Reading Is Fundamental – Research Is Critical)
6. **Leaders Are Made, Not Born** – (Leadership Skills Are Developed, Not Automatically There)
7. **Be Accountable** – (Make Sure People Can Count On You, Keep Your Word)
8. **Use Obstacles as Motivation** – (Your Reaction to Obstacles/Failures Determine Your success)
9. **Truthfully Speaking** – (Use Every Conversation As Practice To Increase Your Speaking Skills)
10. **Build Your A-Team** – (God, Mentors, Contacts, Encouragement, Support)
11. **Live On 5th Avenue** – (Multiple Streams Of Income)
12. **Just Do It** – (Take Small Steps Towards Your Goal Each Day)

These motivational topics were developed by J. Success during the summer of 2002. These 12 topics are the essential qualities that entrepreneurs must possess in order to realize their full potential and leadership qualities.

Which of the twelve "Motivational Topics" do you possess?

☐ 1	☐ 2	☐ 3	☐ 4	☐ 5	☐ 6
☐ 7	☐ 8	☐ 9	☐ 10	☐ 11	☐ 12

If you possess all twelve of those topics then congratulations, you are on your way to being a great entrepreneur and person in life, if you are missing some of those topics, write below how you can obtain those skills.

_____

_____

_____

_____

_____

Qualities of Successful People

Successful people most often exhibit these qualities:
- High levels of **optimism** and **confidence**
- **Vision** and passion in their dreams and convictions
- Surround themselves with other **like-minded** people
- Highly **resourceful**, **creative** and **inventive**
- **Seize opportunities** and create their own whenever possible
- Know what **motivates them** and have a strong sense of **personal identity**
- Spend a substantial amount of time on **introspection** and **self-discovery**
- **Refuse** to let other people dictate how they should live
- Take **responsibility** for their **happiness**
- Spin **challenges** into their greatest motivators—and sometimes biggest advantages
- Take control and ownership of their lives and careers early on, and never let go

Optimism – A tendency to expect the best possible outcome or dwell on the most hopeful aspects of a situation

Confidence – A feeling of assurance, especially of self-assurance

Vision – The manner in which one sees or conceives of something

Passion – Boundless enthusiasm

Resourceful – the ability to utilize whatever they can obtain to reach their goals

Creative – Characterized by originality and expressiveness; imaginative

Motivate – To provide with an incentive; move to action; impel

Personal Identity – the distinct personality of an individual regarded as a persisting entity

Introspection – Contemplation of one's own thoughts, feelings and sensations; self-examination

Responsibility – The state of being responsible, accountable, or answerable, as for a trust, debt or obligation

Happiness – Good luck; good fortune; prosperity

Challenges – A test of one's abilities or resources in a demanding but stimulating undertaking

Definitions were taken from *"The American Heritage Dictionary of the English Language, Fourth Edition"*

Qualities of Successful People

What qualities of successful people do you have?

_____

_____

_____

_____

What are your dreams and convictions?

_____

_____

_____

_____

Do you surround yourself with like-minded people? Yes   No   If Yes, then who?

_____

_____

_____

_____

Are you resourceful, creative and inventive? Give examples:

_____

_____

_____

_____

Do you seize and create opportunities? Give examples:

_____

_____

_____

_____

What motivates you?

_____

_____

_____

_____

What dictates how you live now? (work, school, family, bills, excuses...)

_____

_____

_____

_____

Are you happy? If not, do you see it in your future?

_____

_____

_____

_____

Are you ready to take control of your life?

_____

_____

_____

_____

Success is an inside job. Les Brown said "Most people are six inches away from success, that's the space between your ears." If you can't believe that you will be successful then you never will be. The hardest thing in life is not to achieve success, it's to believe that you can do it.

Here are some mistakes that business owners make when starting a business. Make sure you don't repeat these errors:

1.	Misjudging the market	6.	Setting price to low or to high
2.	Not having a business plan	7.	Choosing wrong partners
3.	Miscalculating the capital needed	8.	Not considering legal aspects
4.	Underestimating the time required	9.	Not understanding employee issues
5.	Not having adequate business skills	10.	Choosing wrong location

Networking

Networking: Networking is building relationships

Why is it important?
Networking is part of the process of developing your business. Your business depends on your relationships with people and other businesses. Since one should always be working on building meaningful relationships, they should always be networking. Networking is not for the shy, if you have problems with meeting people then there are other ways to network. The most effective way to network is to plan, pay attention, suggest and follow up.

Plan – Plan to meet as many people as possible, bring your marketing materials that can easily be exchanged such as business cards.
Pay Attention – Pay attention to what the person is saying. The ability to listen is very important in business, if you pay attention and repeat important things back to the person then you show your genuine interest.
Present – Present yourself and your company to the person, an elevator pitch is a very good way to do this. Make sure your appearance is complimentary to what you are going to say, many people first impression of you is within the first five seconds of seeing you.
Follow up – After the exchange of information and the realization that this person is beneficial to you or that you are beneficial to them, follow up with them and establish an open line of communication for any business endeavors that you all might pursue.

Develop an elevator pitch to describe your business

Elevator pitch – An elevator pitch is a 10 – 20 second summary of your business. It usually consists of your name, the name of your business and what your business does. It is called an elevator pitch because it is supposed to be a pitch that can be stated in the time it takes an elevator to get from the first floor to the third floor.

_____

_____

Places to network
- Personal Network – who do you know
- Internet – Develop a website that markets you and your business, use email to contact people
- Local Groups – Chamber of Commerce, Trade organizations
- Networking Events – these events are setup to increase networking opportunities.
- Anywhere – anywhere that is appropriate is a chance to network, ask questions and get to know the people where you are. You never know who you are sitting next to or who just walked past you.

Networking Tips
- Be sincere and follow Up
- The more people you help the richer you will be
- Network with a diverse group of people
- Be credible, your word is your bond

Networking Skills

Here are the top 10 skills of a very good networker.

1. Networks always. Master networkers are never off duty. Networking is so natural to them that they can be found networking in the grocery store line, at the doctor's office and while picking the kids up from school, as well as at the chamber mixers and networking meetings.

2. Sincere. Insincerity is like a cake without frosting! You can offer the help, the thanks, the listening ear, but if you aren't sincerely interested in the other person, they'll know it! Those who have developed successful networking skills convey their sincerity at every turn. One of the best ways to develop this trait is to give the individual with whom you're developing a referral relationship your undivided attention.

3. Follows up on referrals. This was ranked as the No. 1 trait of successful networkers. If you present an opportunity, whether it's a simple piece of information, a special contact or a qualified business referral, to someone who consistently fails to follow up successfully, it's no secret that you'll eventually stop wasting your time with this person.

4. Positive attitude. A consistently negative attitude makes people dislike being around you and drives away referrals; a positive attitude makes people want to associate and cooperate with you. Positive business professionals are like magnets. Others want to be around them and will send their friends, family and associates to them.

5. Enthusiastic/motivated. Think about the people you know. Who gets the most referrals? People who show the most motivation, right? It's been said that the best sales characteristic is enthusiasm. To be respected within our networks, we at least need to sell ourselves with enthusiasm. Once we've done an effective job of selling ourselves, we'll be able to reap the reward of seeing our contacts sell us to others! That's motivation in and of itself!

6. Trustworthy. When you refer one person to another, you're putting your reputation on the line. You have to be able to trust your referral partner and be trusted in return. Neither you nor anyone else will refer a contact or valuable information to someone who can't be trusted to handle it well.

7. Good listening skills. Our success as networkers depends on how well we can listen and learn. The faster you and your networking partner learn what you need to know about each other, the faster you'll establish a valuable relationship. Communicate well, and listen well.

8. Enjoys helping. Helping others can be done in a variety of ways, from literally showing up to help with an office move to clipping a helpful and interesting article and mailing it to an associate or client. Master networkers keep their eyes and ears open for opportunities to advance other people's interests whenever they can.

9. Thanks people. Gratitude is sorely lacking in today's business world. Expressing gratitude to business associates and clients is just another building block in the cultivation of relationships that will lead to increased referrals. People like to refer others to business professionals that go above and beyond. Thanking others at every opportunity will help you stand out from the crowd.

10. Works their network. It's not net-sit or net-eat, it's net-work, and master networkers don't let any opportunity to work their networks pass them by. They manage their contacts with contact management software, organize their e-mail address files and carry their referral partners' business cards as well as their own. They set up appointments to get better acquainted with new contacts so that they can learn as much about them as possible so that they can truly become part of each other's networks.

Motivational Topics Worksheet

1. **Attitude Is Everything** –

2. **You Control Your Destiny** –

3. **Develop A "Whatever It Takes" Attitude** –

4. **Develop A Plan And Write It Down** –

5. **Self Development** –

6. **Leaders Are Made, Not Born** –

7. **Be Accountable** –

8. **Use Obstacles as Motivation** –

9. **Truthfully Speaking** –

10. **Build Your A-Team** –

11. **Live On 5th Avenue** –

12. **Just Do It** –

A. (God, Mentors, Contacts, Encouragement, Support)
B. (Reading Is Fundamental – Research Is Critical)
C. (Success Is A State Of Mind)
D. (Take Small Steps Towards Your Goal Each Day)
E. (Make Sure People Can Count On You, Keep Your Word)
F. (You Have To Know Where You Are Going)
G. (Use Every Conversation As Practice To Increase Your Speaking Skills)
H. (Multiple Streams Of Income)
I. (Your Reaction to Obstacles/Failures Determine Your success)
J. (To have what you've never had you must do what you've never done)
K. (Successful People Control Their Destinies)
L. (Leadership Skills Are Developed, Not Automatically There)

Part II
Business Planning

Most people take "*life as it comes*", successful people take "*control of their life*".

- J. Success –

Business Concepts

Ideas are the beginning of business concepts. Business concepts are ideas that have begun the process of becoming business ventures. The turning point comes when your idea changes

> **From**   What it is you want to do
>
> **To**   What the market needs and how you will get it to them

Journalists always ask the same five questions when they are putting together a story: **who, what, when, where and why**. These same five questions apply when you are trying to develop your business concept. In order to become a successful entrepreneur, **you should be able to clearly describe your business**. Let's do an example.

Business: Digital One Technology Inc. is a web design and training company that was started in August 2002. We focus on small businesses and educational institutions to provide our training and web design services. Digital One Technology Inc. offers professional services at economical prices. We also offer training programs that focus on technology and entrepreneurship and that is what sets us apart from the competition. In the future we plan to expand our offerings to individuals by creating a conventional and online school to offer our training services. Currently we sell all of our services via our website which is located at www.d1-t.com. Digital One Technology Inc. promotes it products via email, mailings, word of mouth and most importantly, networking.

Who buys the product or services offered by this company?

_____

_____

_____

What does the product or service consist of?

_____

_____

_____

When was this product or service first offered?

_____

_____

_____

_____

Where can customers get this product or service?

_____

_____

_____

Why do customers purchase this product or service; what sets this company apart?

_____

_____

Who will buy your product or service?

_____

_____

What does your product or service consist of?

_____

_____

_____

_____

When will you be offering this product or service?

_____

_____

_____

Where will you be offering this product or service?

_____

_____

Why are you offering this product or service/ what need or want are you fulfilling?

_____

_____

_____

_____

Features vs. Benefits

When you are considering your product or service, you want to make sure that you highlight the features and benefits of your product or services.

Feature – What the product or service does

Benefit – Why the customers would buy the product or service

Features	Benefits

Vision and Mission Statements

No matter how many changes that your company goes through or how many different products/services you add, there are certain ideals that your company should adhere to that provide guidance in the decisions and focus of the company. These unchanging principles form the business vision and should be expressed in the company mission statement and vision statement.

The mission statement should project your companies' values, purpose and vision. The values of your company should not waver according to the industry or fads. The purpose of your company is what sets your company apart from other companies. Each company has a purpose and a way to make a profit and that should be clearly stated.

The vision statement of your company should reflect the goals and objectives that your company will achieve. These goals should be high reaching and reap high rewards. Short-term goals should not be included here, only long term goals that will take your company to the higher levels of achievement.

Examples		
Company Values	**Company Purpose**	**Company Vision**
1. Excellent customer service 2. Creativity 3. Integrity	To teach people how to create their own businesses in one day.	To teach people to take control of their future through knowledge and empowerment.

Your Company		
Company Values	**Company Purpose**	**Company Vision**
1. 2. 3.		

Now lets create your mission statement and vision statement for your company. Remember, the ideal mission statement and vision statement is usually no longer then a sentence long and it gets right to the point. The ideal statement will define a clear direction for the company.

Mission Statement Example: Microsoft's mission is to enable people and businesses throughout the world to realize their full potential through technology.

_____

_____

Vision Statement Example: Microsoft's vision is to empower people through great software anytime, anyplace and on any device.

_____

_____

Opportunity Recognition

Opportunity recognition is a skill that every entrepreneur should have. If you do not know how to recognize an opportunity then you will not be in business very long. The best entrepreneurs are able to recognize opportunities before other people and therefore act upon them. Let's think of some entrepreneurs that took advantage of opportunities.
- Bill Gates and software (Microsoft)
- Michael Dell and the personal computer (Dell)
- Pierre Omidyar and e-commerce (Ebay)
- Larry Page and Sergey Brin and search engines (Google)

What is an opportunity?
- An opportunity is a risk that will have a positive outcome.
- An opportunity is a need backed by a demand in the marketplace.

What gives rise to opportunities?
There are a variety of circumstances that can give rise to an opportunity.

o Trends	o Problems
o Industries	o Helping people
o Catastrophic events	o Innovation
o Advancement in technology	o Creativity

If you can recognize and take advantage of the circumstances that give rise to opportunities, then you will definitely be successful. Always look for and recognize different opportunities because they are all around you.

Where are opportunities?
Everywhere!!!!! Take a look around your community, home, places of leisure, venues, internet and other various places. Think of how you either can improve what you already see or fill a need that has not been filled or identified. Think outside the box and try to see opportunities that others overlook.

Assessment of an opportunity – when you want to pursue an opportunity, there are some assessments that you should consider prior to making a decision.

Real:	Is it really an opportunity? Is it a want people will pay for? Is it something people see as a problem?
Competition:	Is anyone else doing it or thinking about it?
Enduring:	How long is this window of opportunity open? Is it a trend or fad?
Specific Information:	Have you specifically defined the opportunity so that you can focus on one area?
Market:	Is there a market that awaits this opportunity? Are there people that are willing to pay for this opportunity?
Experience:	Are you experienced enough to take advantage of this opportunity?
Product:	Can you come up with a product or service to fulfill this opportunity?
Comparison:	Is this opportunity better than other opportunities that you have identified?
Risks:	What are the obstacles that you will need to overcome?

<u>Opportunity Recognition</u>

Let's write down an opportunity and assess it.

The opportunity is:

_____

_____

_____

Real:	
Competition:	
Enduring:	
Specific Information:	
Market:	
Experience:	
Product:	
Comparison:	
Risks:	

Marketing

Marketing - identifying unmet needs; producing products and services to meet those needs: and pricing, distributing, and promoting those products and services to produce a profit.

Many companies have had great products but poor marketing and therefore their products have gone unnoticed. There are many types of marketing that you can utilize for your product or service, located below are some that you should become familiar with.

1. **Paid Advertising** – This advertising consists of paying for a particular type of advertising. These include radio, television, newspaper, magazines and catalogs. This type of marketing should be broken down by area (local, regional, national) and potential audience.

2. **Promotion** – This type of marketing consist of sales, discounts, coupons, special deals and major campaigns. This marketing tool is designed to move more products. However, make sure that you have calculated the costs prior to considering a promotion.

3. **Public Relations** – This type of marketing is usually considered free marketing. Companies that usually make use of public relations usually distribute press releases and other releases to outlets that will get the word out.

4. **Trade Shows** – This marketing tool is vital to many types of businesses. Trade shows are usually major showcases for your products with many potential customers all in one location.

5. **Direct Mail** – This marketing tool usually takes the most effort and generates a low ROI (return on investment). Direct mail uses postcards, flyers, letters of introduction and other mailed advertisements that get the word out about a particular company. Marketing companies state the direct mail response is around 3%. Therefore for every 100 items you mail, expect 3 to generate a response.

6. **Marketing Materials** – These marketing tools could consist of brochures, point of purchase displays, and inserts with other products. These materials are used to explain your product or service in detail and are strategically placed to achieve the best results.

7. **Online Marketing** – These marketing tools consist of email blasts, online banners, pop-ups, Adwords, and most importantly, websites. Online marketing is a 24/7 type of marketing that can reach many potential customers. The Internet's main purpose is to move information quickly and all companies should take advantage of its capabilities.

8. **Word of Mouth** – By far the most important and significant marketing tool. Customers will always talk about a company and the products or services it offers. You want to make sure that all customers that talk about your company have good things to say. An old saying goes "If you give good service a person will tell another. If you give bad service a person will tell several."

Marketing

What is your product or service?

_____

_____

What marketing tools would help you most with your business?

☐ Paid Advertising   ☐ Promotion   ☐ Public Relations   ☐ Trade Shows

☐ Direct Mail   ☐ Marketing Materials   ☐ Online Marketing   ☐ Word of
Mouth

How will you utilize the marketing tools that you chose?

_____

_____

_____

_____

_____

Logo
A great logo can make or break a business. Many people know companies before they even see their name because of their logo. A good logo should reflect every aspect of your company in a graphic representation. You want to bring some type of positive response from potential customers when they see your logo. Have you developed a logo? If so draw it here, if not then use this space to come up with ideas. (My company logos are given as examples).

Digital One Technology Inc.   Digital One Learning   My Success Academy Inc.

<u>Marketing Strategy</u>

When you are trying to figure out who your market is you should ask yourself, "Who are my customers? Who will buy my product?" Most potential entrepreneurs and established small business owners either have no idea who will buy from them, or they assume that 'everyone' will. Assumptions like this can lead to wrong decisions, wrong pricing, wrong marketing strategy and ultimately, business failure.

The most successful small businesses understand that (usually) only a limited number of people will buy their product or service. The task then becomes determining, as closely as possible, exactly who those people are, and 'targeting' the business's marketing efforts toward them. You, too, can build a better, stronger business, by identifying and serving a particular customer group – your target market.

Next, you need to understand that people purchase products or services for three basic reasons:

- o To satisfy basic needs
- o To solve problems
- o To make themselves feel good

Make sure that your product/service meets at least one of these three reasons. The more reasons that you can meet the more revenue that your product/service will generate.

What reason will people buy your product?
- ☐ To satisfy basic needs
- ☐ To solve problems
- ☐ To make themselves feel good

How will your product meet this reason?

_____

_____

_____

Marketing Strategy (cont'd)

Business to Consumer

The first task you'll need to do is research the 'demographics' of your market (potential customers), and divide it into market segments. This information should be available to you via the library, village hall or Chamber of Commerce – and the more detail you can get, the better.

Check the demographic answer that best describes your market (potential customers).

Age: ☐ children ☐ teens ☐ young ☐ middle ☐ elderly

Gender: ☐ male ☐ female

Education: ☐ high school ☐ college ☐ university

Income: ☐ low ☐ medium ☐ high

Marital status: ☐ single ☐ married ☐ divorced

Ethnic and/or religious background: _____

Family life cycle: ☐ newly married ☐ married for 10 – 20 years ☐ with or ☐ without children.

Lifestyle: ☐ conservative ☐ exciting ☐ trendy ☐ economical

Social class: ☐ lower ☐ middle ☐ upper

Opinion: ☐ easily led or ☐ opinionated

Activities and interests: ☐ sports ☐ physical fitness ☐ shopping ☐ books

Attitudes and beliefs: ☐ environmentalist ☐ security conscious.

Business to Business

If you are a B2B company, you'll also need to consider the types of industries available to you, and their number of employees, annual sales volume, location, and company stability.

Check the demographic answer that best describes your market (potential customers).

Number of employees: ☐ 1-50 ☐ 51-100 ☐ 101-500 ☐ 501-1000 ☐ 1000+

Annual sales volume: ☐ $1 – $50,000 ☐ $50,001 - $100,000 ☐ $100,001 - $500,000 ☐ $500,001 - $1,000,000 ☐ $1,000,000+

Location: ☐ local ☐ regional ☐ national ☐ international

Company stability: ☐ very good ☐ good ☐ okay ☐ bad

E-commerce capabilities: ☐ highly technical ☐ technical ☐ not very technical

Marketing Strategy

Niche Market - A niche market is a focused, targetable portion of a market.

By definition, aa business that focuses on a niche market is addressing a need for a product or service that is not being addressed by mainstream providers. You can think of a niche market as a narrowly defined group of potential customers.

Why should you bother to establish a niche market? Because of the great advantage of being alone there other small businesses may not be aware of your particular niche market, and large businesses won't want to bother with it.

The trick to capitalizing on a niche market is to find or develop a market niche that has customers who are accessible, that is growing fast enough and that is not owned by an established vendor already.

Here are examples of niche markets:
- Minority children between the ages of 5 and 7
- Asians
- Women in their twenties
- African-American men aged 30 – 39
- Teenagers

What are possible niche markets for your product or service? (To identify a good niche market, take your market and break it down into a specific niche that will maximize your results.)

_____

_____

_____

_____

_____

<u>Industry Overview</u>

In order to be successful in business you need to be very aware of your industry and the trends. Prior to starting your business you should do what's commonly referred to as "due diligence". A part of "due diligence" consists of knowing your industry and being aware of the upcoming and past tendencies. For example, a computer training business owner would need to be aware of new technologies, upgrades to current technologies, new training standards as well as developing technologies. With this knowledge the business owner could develop a company that meets the needs of the industry and also adapt his business to the ever-changing computer technology industry.

There are a variety of sources that you can use to find out information on your industry. The most valuable source of information is the Internet. You can go to any of the many search engines and type in the name of your industry into and you will get many sites that return free information about your industry.

When you find information about your industry check its date and determine whether or not the information is current enough to be valid and write down the date and source of the information, as you'll need to cite your information sources in the business plan.

Here are some questions to help you complete your industry overview:

1. On the Internet, go to a search engine (www.yahoo.com, www.google.com) and type in your industry (ex: computer training industry) and check out three sites about your industry. What have you learned about your industry?

_____

_____

_____

_____

_____

_____

_____

_____

_____

_____

<u>Industry Overview</u>

1. What industry are you in? _____

_____

2. What is the size of your industry?

_____

_____

3. What sectors does this industry include?

_____

_____

4. Who are the major players in this industry?

_____

_____

5. What are the markets and customers for this industry?

_____

_____

6. What are the industry's estimated sales this year? Last year?

_____

_____

_____

7. What national/economic trends have affected this industry and how?

_____

_____

_____

8. What national/economic trends might affect it in the future and how?

_____

_____

9. What is the long-term outlook for this industry?

_____

_____

Competitive Analysis

In order to develop a true marketing strategy, it should address how a business will compete against other businesses. A good way to focus on this section is to present the most directly competitive products or companies, introduce a few key competitive points (price, size, number of stores, availability of colors and so on), and then produce a table that shows how you stack up against the competition.

When you're putting together a competitive comparison, make sure you choose the largest and most direct competitors. Pick two or three competitors and show how your products or services match up and outperform the major competition.

Example:

Company	Price	Convenience	Customer service
Dell	$399	Customized orders	24 hour support
HP/Compaq	$899	Preset orders	9-5 support
Bob's Computers	$199	Customized orders	24 hour online support

The **Bob's Computers** shows that it can compete with the major players according to what it is offering.

Let's do a competitive analysis for your business. Fill in the companies and the competitive points that you want to showcase.

Company				

Can you compete with your competitors? ☐ Yes   ☐ No

Are there any changes within your company that you need to make so that you can better compete with your competitors?

_____

_____

_____

Core Competencies and Challenges

Core Competencies
The core competencies section of a business plan focuses on the unique competitive advantages your business has. You want to focus on the strengths of your company that will play a major role in your success. These strengths should be easily visible and understood by your market and should distinguish you from your competition. Make sure you talk about how your features will benefit the customer. Be clear, concise and stick to the facts.

Write down three of your core competencies.

1. _____

    _____

2. _____

    _____

3. _____

    _____

Challenges
The challenges section of a business plan focuses on the unique challenges your business has. You want to focus on the challenges of your company and identify a solution. These challenges should be easily visible and understood by your market. Make sure you talk about how your challenges will be resolved and how the solution will benefit the customer. Be clear, concise and stick to the facts.

Write down three of your challenges.

1. _____

    _____

2. _____

    _____

3. _____

    _____

<u>Business Structures</u>

<u>Now that I know what I want to do, how do I set up my business?</u>

Well there are quite a few business structures that we explain in this workbook, but we focus on corporations. Business structures are the legal formation of your company. In order to properly run a business your business must have one of the structures listed below.

Sole Proprietorship – A sole proprietorship is an unincorporated business that is owned by one individual. It is the simplest form of business organization to start and maintain. The business has no existence apart from you, the owner. Its liabilities are your personal liabilities and you undertake the risks of the business for all assets owned, whether used in the business or personally owned. You include the income and expenses of the business on your own tax return.

Limited/General Partnership – A partnership is the relationship existing between two or more persons who join to carry on a trade or business. Each person contributes money, property, labor or skill, and expects to share in the profits and losses of the business.

Limited Liability Company – LLCs are popular because, similar to a corporation, owners have limited personal liability for the debts and actions of the LLC. Other features of LLCs are more like a partnership, providing management flexibility and the benefit of pass-through taxation. Owners of an LLC are called members. Since most states do not restrict ownership, members may include individuals, corporations, other LLCs and foreign entities. There is no maximum number of members. Most states also permit "single member" LLCs, those having only one owner

C Corporation – A C-corporation is a legal entity created under state law. A form of organization where ownership is vested in the stockholders. A corporation is an official being, invisible, intangible, and existing in contemplation of the law.

S Corporation – A S-corporation is a legal entity created under state law. A form of organization where ownership is vested in the stockholders but the S-corporation can only have 75 stockholders. On their tax returns, the S corporation's shareholders include their share of the corporation's separately stated items of income, deduction, loss, and credit, and their share of non-separately stated income or loss. A corporation is an official being, invisible, intangible, and existing in contemplation of the law.

Definitions of business structures obtained from the IRS website.

Update: The main question often asked when looking at business structures is what's the difference between corporations and limited liability companies. In a nutshell, the answer is paperwork. Corporations have to legally document meetings between shareholders and directors and provide that documentation. LLC's are not bound legally (yet) to document meetings as strictly as corporations. Everything else is pretty much similar. Registration for both requires articles (articles of incorporation for corporation, articles of organization for LLC), Taxation for both can either use a separate for or flow through taxation, Setup for both can use one person normally and both have limited liability by being recognized as separate entities.

Business Structures and Taxes

Taxes

One of the main reasons for various business structures are the tax purposes. Listed below are the ways taxes are applied to the various business structures. According to the IRS website, here are the taxes that each structure is liable for and the forms that should be filled out.

Sole Proprietorship – taxes at individual tax rate and has very few tax benefits.
- Income Tax – 1040 and Schedule C or CEZ (Schedule F for farm businesses)
- Self-employment tax – 1040 and Schedule SE
- Estimated tax – 1040ES
- Federal unemployment tax (FUTA)
  - 941 (943 for farm employees), 940 or 940EZ, 8109

Limited/General Partnership – A partnership must file an annual information return to report the income, deductions, gains, losses etc., form its operations, but it does not pay income tax. Instead, it "passes through" any profits or losses to its partners. Each partner includes his or her share of the partnership's income or loss on his or her tax return. Partners are not employees and should not be issued a Form W-2. The partnership must furnish copies of Schedule K-1 (Form 1065) to the partners by the date Form 1065 is required to be filed, including extensions.
- Income Tax – 1065
- Employment Taxes – Social Security and Medicare
- Federal unemployment tax (FUTA)
  - 941 (943 for farm employees), 940 or 940EZ, 8109

C/S Corporation – Because a corporation is a separate legal entity from its owners, the company itself is taxed on all profits that it cannot deduct as business expenses. Generally, taxable profits consist of money kept in the company to cover expenses or expansion (called "retained earnings") and profits that are distributed to the owners (shareholders) as dividends. To reduce taxable profits, a corporation can deduct its business expenses -- basically, any money the corporation spends in the legitimate pursuit of profit.
- Income Tax – 1120 (1120S for S corp)
- Estimated Tax – 1120W and 8109
- Employment Taxes – Social Security and Medicare
- Federal unemployment tax (FUTA)
  - 941 (943 for farm employees), 940 or 940EZ, 8109
- S Corporation Shareholders – 1040 and Schedule E

Limited Liability Company - An LLC is what the IRS calls a "pass-through entity," like a partnership or sole proprietorship. All of the profits and losses of the LLC "pass through" the business to the LLC owners (called members), who report this information on their personal tax returns. The LLC itself does not pay federal income taxes, but some states do charge the LLC itself an annual state tax. Any LLC can be treated like a corporation for tax purposes by filing IRS Form 8832 and checking the corporate tax treatment box on the form.
- If the only member of the LLC is an individual, the LLC income and expenses are reported on form 1040 and schedule C,E or F.
- If the only member of the LLC is a corporation, then the LLC income and expenses are reported on the 1120 or 1120S.
- If you prefer to file as a corporation instead of a "disregarded entity" Form 8832 must be submitted.
- If you prefer to file as a partnership instead of a "disregarded entity" Form 1065 must be submitted.

Corporation Benefits

Why does J. Success suggest corporations and LLC's?

Limited Liability – The liability of a firm's owners for no more capital than they have invested in the business. Essentially, the legal separation of ownership and liability means that a stockholder can lose no more than he or she has paid for the shares of ownership regardless of the firm's financial obligations. Limited liability is one of the major advantages of organizing a business as a corporation.

Piercing the Corporate Veil – A court may pierce through the veil of liability protection if the corporation does not follow proper corporation formalities, if it is undercapitalized, or if it can be shown that it is a sham that was set up to defraud. Make sure that you follow the corporate formalities in order to not have your corporate veil pierced, make sure you have annual meetings with recorded minutes, distribute stock, file annual reports, keep good financial records, and file your taxes.

Tax Deductions – One of the major reasons for starting a corporation is to minimize your taxes. As stated earlier a corporation can deduct its business expenses -- basically, any money the corporation spends in the legitimate pursuit of profit.

• Auto expenses	• Bank service charges
• Startup expenses	• Business association dues
• Education expenses	• Business gifts
• Legal And professional fees	• Business-related magazines and books
• Bad debts	• Casualty and theft losses
• Business entertaining	• Consultant fees
• Travel	• Office supplies
• New equipment	• Online computer services related to business
• Interest	• Parking and meters
• Moving expenses	• Petty cash funds
• Software	• Postage
• Charitable contributions	• Promotion and publicity
• Taxes	• Seminars and trade shows
• Advertising and promotion	• Taxi and bus fare
• Audiotapes and videotapes related to business skills	• Telephone calls away from the business

What is the best business structure for your business?
☐ Sole Proprietorship   ☐ Partnership   ☐ Corporation   ☐ LLC

Why is this structure the best for you? What are the benefits?

_____

_____

Business Formation Process

Here are the business structures and the general process needed to form them. I have used the states of Illinois and California as examples because those are the states that I do the most business in. Each state has a slightly different process so make sure you check that out before beginning you process

Sole Proprietorship:
- SS4 document for FEIN number (call IRS 866-816-2065) or you can use your Social Security number
- Take FEIN number to bank for business account (optional)
- NUC-1 Illinois Business Registration (optional for IL only)
- File Assumed Name registration with a newspaper for at least two weeks
- *File the Schedule C form along with 1040 for taxes at the end of the year

Limited Liability Partnership
- SS4 document for FEIN number (call IRS 866-816-2065)
- Take FEIN number to bank for business account
- UPA 1101 Illinois Statement of Qualification (IL only)
- NUC-1 Illinois Business Registration (IL only)
- LLP-1 Limited Liability Partnership registration (CA only)
- *File the (form 1065 for IL, form 565 for CA) plus schedule K-1 and 1040 for taxes at end of the year

Limited Liability Company:
- SS4 document for FEIN number (call IRS 866-816-2065)
- LLC-5.5 Article of Organization (IL only)
- NUC-1 Illinois Business Registration (IL only)
- Take Articles of Organization to Bank for business account
- *Each year you have to fill out an annual report (IL report with Sec. of State, CA report with Franchise tax board)
- *For personal taxation file business taxes on personal return, for corporate taxation file form 8832. (also file form 568 for CA)

C Corporation:

- SS4 document for FEIN number (call IRS 866-816-2065)
- Articles of Incorporation with Secretary of State
- NUC-1 Illinois Business Registration (IL only)
- File County Registration Document with county of incorporation (IL only)
- Take Articles of Incorporation to bank for business account
- *Each year you have to fill out an annual report (IL report with Sec. of State, CA report with Franchise tax board)
- *Each year you have to file Federal 1120S taxes (IL state form is 1120, CA state form is 100)

For S Corporation do all the above as well as:

- Form 2553 to declare S Corporation status with the IRS
- *Each year you have to fill out an annual report (IL report with Sec. of State, CA report with Franchise tax board)
- *Each year you have to file Federal 1120S taxes (IL state form is 1120S, CA state form is 100S)

Benefits of Each Structure

	Corporation (C,S)	LLC (Limited Liability Company)	Partnership (Limited, General)	Sole Proprietorship
Startup process	• FEIN number • Articles of incorporation filed with state • Annual meetings required • Bylaws need to be documented • Register business for state taxes (usually state dept. of revenue) • S Corp requires Form 2553 to be filed within 75 days of incorporation	• FEIN number • Articles filed with state • Annual meetings • Register business for state taxes (usually state dept. of revenue)	• FEIN number • LP-1 filed with state for limited partnership • Partnership agreement • Register business for state taxes (usually state dept. of revenue)	• FEIN number (or use SSN#) • Register DBA name with local newspaper
Liability for business issues and commitments	• Business is liable, owners are not personally liable for business issues and commitments	• Business is liable, owners are not personally liable for business issues and commitments	• Partners are personally liable for all business issues and commitments	• Owner is personally liable for all business issues and commitments
Who Owns business and makes business decisions	• Board of Directors make decisions • Shareholders own business based on stock	• Any member of LLC	• Any partner	• Sole proprietor
Tax rates	• C-Corp is taxed on profits after the deductions • S-Corp profits flow through to individual shareholders tax forms	• Depends on taxation process chosen, if individual then it flows through to members individually, if corporate then they are taxed as a corporation	• Individual tax rate	• Individual tax rate
How many people does it take to start this structure	• Some states allow just one person, others require at least two	• Some states allow just one person, others require at least two	• At least two partners	• One person
If owner becomes deceased	• Business continues to function as normal	• Business dissolves unless members vote to continue	• Business dissolves unless previous agreement states continuation	• Business is dissolved

Financial Data

The financial plan section determines whether or not your business idea is viable, and is a key component in determining whether or not your business plan is going to be able to attract any investment in your business idea. Here are the financial sections that we will focus on:

1. Personal Financial Statement
2. Startup Costs
3. Break-even Analysis
4. Income Statement
5. Cash Flow Projection

1. Personal Financial Statement or Balance Sheet

The Balance Sheet/Personal Financial Statement presents a picture of you or your business' net worth at a particular point in time. It summarizes all the financial data about you or your business, breaking that data into three categories: assets, liabilities and equity.

2. Startup Costs

All the costs of getting your business up and running go into the start up expenses category.

These expenses may include:
- Business registration fees
- Business licensing and permits
- Starting inventory
- Rent deposits
- Down payments on property
- Down payments on equipment
- Utility setup fees

This is just a sampling of startup expenses; your own list will probably expand as soon as you start writing them down.

Operating expenses are the costs of keeping your business running. Think of these as the things you're going to have to pay each month. Your list of operating expenses may include:
- Salaries (yours and staff salaries)
- Rent or mortgage payments
- Telecommunications
- Utilities
- Raw materials
- Storage
- Distribution
- Promotion
- Loan payments
- Office supplies
- Maintenance

Once again, this is just a partial list to get you going. Once you have your operating expenses list complete, the total will show you what it will cost to keep your business running each month.

Multiply this number by six, and you have a six month estimate of your operating expenses. Then add this to the total of your start up expenses list, and you'll have a ballpark figure for your complete startup costs.

3. Break-Even Analysis

The Break-even Analysis lets you determine what you need to sell, monthly or annually, to cover your costs of doing business--your break-even point.

It is frequently mistaken for the payback period, the time it takes to recover an investment. There are variations on break-even that make some people think we have it wrong. The one we do use is the most common, the most universally accepted, but not the only one possible.

It depends on the concept of fixed costs, a hard idea to swallow. Technically, a break-even analysis defines fixed costs as those costs that would continue even if you went broke. Instead, you may want to use your regular running fixed costs, including payroll and normal expenses. This will give you a better insight on financial realities. We call that "burn rate" these post-Internet days.

It depends on averaging your per-unit variable cost and per-unit revenue over the whole business. However, whether we like it or not, this table is a mainstay of financial analysis. You may choose to leave it out, but really, a business plan would not be complete without it. And, although there are some other ways to do a Break-even Analysis, this is the most standard.

The Break-even Analysis depends on three key assumptions:

Average per-unit sales price (per-unit revenue):
This is the price that you receive per unit of sales. Take into account sales discounts and special offers. Get this number from your Sales Forecast. For non-unit based businesses, make the per-unit revenue $1 and enter your costs as a percent of a dollar. The most common questions about this input relate to averaging many different products into a single estimate. The analysis requires a single number, and if you build your Sales Forecast first, then you will have this number. You are not alone in this, the vast majority of businesses sell more than one item, and have to average for their Break-even Analysis.

Average per-unit cost:
This is the incremental cost, or variable cost, of each unit of sales. If you buy goods for resale, this is what you paid, on average, for the goods you sell. If you sell a service, this is what it costs you, per dollar of revenue or unit of service delivered, to deliver that service. If you are using a Units-Based Sales Forecast table (for manufacturing and mixed business types), you can project unit costs from the Sales Forecast table. If you are using the basic Sales Forecast table for retail, service and distribution businesses, use a percentage estimate, e.g., a retail store running a 50% margin would have a per-unit cost of .5, and a per-unit revenue of 1.

Monthly fixed costs:
Technically, a Break-Even Analysis defines fixed costs as costs that would continue even if you went broke. Instead, we recommend that you use your regular running fixed costs, including payroll and normal expenses (total monthly Operating Expenses). This will give you a better insight on financial realities. If averaging and estimating is difficult, use your Profit and Loss table to calculate a working fixed cost estimate—it will be a rough estimate, but it will provide a useful input for a conservative Break-even Analysis.

The Break-Even Analysis depends on assumptions made for average per-unit revenue, average per-unit cost, and fixed costs. These are rarely exact. We recommend that you do the break-even table twice: first, with educated guesses for assumptions, as part of the initial assessment, and later on, using your detailed Sales Forecast and Profit and Loss numbers. Both are valid uses

4. Income Statement

The Income Statement shows your revenues, expenses and profit for a particular period. It's a snapshot of your business that shows whether or not your business is profitable at that point in time.

While established businesses normally produce an Income Statement each fiscal quarter, or even once each fiscal year, for the purposes of the business plan, an Income Statement should be generated more frequently - monthly for the first year.

Annual income statement projection (for five years)
Quarterly income statement projection (for two years)
Monthly income statement projection (for one year)

5. Cash Flow Projection

The Cash Flow Projection shows how cash is expected to flow in and out of your business. For you, it's an important tool for cash flow management, letting you know when your expenditures are too high or when you might want to arrange short term investments to deal with a cash flow surplus. As part of your business plan, a Cash Flow Projection will give you a much better idea of how much capital investment your business idea needs.

For a bank loans officer, the Cash Flow Projection offers evidence that your business is a good credit risk and that there will be enough cash on hand to make your business a good candidate for a line of credit or short term loan.

Do not confuse a Cash Flow Projection with a Cash Flow Statement. The Cash Flow Statement shows how cash has flowed in and out of your business. In other words, it describes the cash flow that has occurred in the past. The Cash Flow Projection shows the cash that is anticipated to be generated or expended over a chosen period of time in the future.

While both types of Cash Flow reports are important business decision-making tools for businesses, we're only concerned with the Cash Flow Projection in the business plan. You will want to show Cash Flow Projections for each month over a one year period as part of the Financial Plan portion of your business plan.

There are three parts to the Cash Flow Projection. The first part details your Cash Revenues. Enter your estimated sales figures for each month. Remember that these are Cash Revenues; you will only enter the sales that are collectible in cash during the specific month you are dealing with.

The second part is your Cash Disbursements. Take the various expense categories from your ledger and list the cash expenditures you actually expect to pay that month for each month.

The third part of the Cash Flow Projection is the Reconciliation of Cash Revenues to Cash Disbursements. As the word "reconciliation" suggests, this section starts with an opening balance which is the carryover from the previous month's operations. The current month's Revenues are added to this balance; the current month's Disbursements are subtracted, and the adjusted cash flow balance is carried over to the next month.

Financing

While poor management is cited most frequently as the reason businesses fail, inadequate or ill-timed financing is a close second. Whether you're starting a business or expanding one, sufficient ready capital is essential. But it is not enough to simply have sufficient financing; knowledge and planning are required to manage it well. These qualities ensure that entrepreneurs avoid common mistakes like securing the wrong type of financing, miscalculating the amount required, or underestimating the cost of borrowing money.

Before inquiring about financing, ask yourself the following:

1. Do you need more capital or can you manage existing cash flow more effectively?

   _____

   _____

2. How do you define your need? Do you need money to expand or as a cushion against risk?

   _____

   _____

3. How urgent is your need? You can obtain the best terms when you anticipate your needs rather than looking for money under pressure.

   _____

   _____

4. How great are your risks? All businesses carry risks, and the degree of risk will affect cost and available financing alternatives.

   _____

   _____

5. In what state of development is the business? Needs are most critical during transitional stages.

   _____

   _____

6. For what purposes will the capital be used? Any lender will require that capital be requested for very specific needs.

   _____

   _____

7. What is the state of your industry? Depressed, stable or growth conditions require different approaches to money needs and sources. Businesses that prosper while others are in decline will often receive better funding terms.

    _____

    _____

8. Is your business seasonal or cyclical? Seasonal needs for financing generally are short term. Loans advanced for cyclical industries such as construction are designed to support a business through depressed periods.

    _____

    _____

9. How strong is your management team? Management is the most important element assessed by money sources.

    _____

    _____

10. Perhaps most importantly, how does your need for financing mesh with your business plan? If you don't have a business plan, make writing one your first priority. All capital sources will want to see your plan for the startup and growth of your business.

    _____

    _____

Financing

Let's take a look at some of the most common financing options for businesses. A good resource for business finance information is http://www.sba.gov/financing/

Loans - Something lent for temporary use, A sum of money lent at interest, a loan made by a bank; to be repaid with interest on or before a fixed date

When financing a startup if you apply for a loan, you have to convince a potential lender or investor that you and your business are sound investments. You have to show that your business will be profitable and that you or whomever you hire will be able to manage the company and not take it under. Generally, a business will need the following documentation to evaluate your loan request:

o   **Business Profile** - A document describing type of business, annual sales, number of employees, length of time in business and ownership.

o   **Loan Request** - A description of how loan funds will be used. Should include purpose, amount and type of loan.

o   **Collateral** - Description of collateral offered to secure the loan, including equity in the business, borrowed funds and available cash.

o   **Business Financial Statements** - Complete financial statements for the past 3 years and current interim financial statements.

o   **Personal Financial Statements** - Statements of owners, partners, officers and stockholders owning 20% or more of the business.

The Small Business Administration is the primary organization for small business financing. They have many loan programs that help businesses get to the level where they can compete with the major companies. Their site is located at http://www.sba.gov/services/financialassistance/index.html.

Grants – Any monetary aid that is given to an individual or small business and does not have to be repaid or returned.

There are many small business grants that are available to you and your business. The best place to look is the Internet. There are many sites that list information related to business grants. This site gives the business grant links for every state http://usgovinfo.about.com/library/weekly/blstategrants.htm

Bootstrapping – The process of developing something without reliance on outside help such as investor money. This is the process by which my first company was financed. When you are bootstrapping, you have an alternate source of income such as a second job that finances the company (and yourself) until it becomes profitable.

Angel Investors/Venture Capitalists – Individuals who invest in businesses looking for a higher return than they would see from more traditional investments. In return for their investment they often are highly involved in the business.

Make sure that if you decide to utilize investors, you are prepared to give up some of the control of your company in exchange for their investment.

Financing

Let's assess your situation and try to come up with some financial options for you.

	1	2	3
1. How is your credit? 1 = bad, 2 = average, 3 = good (*if you have good credit then you can get a loan based on your score)			
2. How long have you been in business? 1 = startup, 2 = 1 year, 3 = 2 or more years			
3. What type of collateral do you have? **(home, car, investments)** 1 = nothing, 2 = car, 3 = home and car			
4. What type of personal financing do you have? **(savings, cash)** 1 = nothing, 2 = some cash, 3 = cash and credit			
5. Do you have a relationship with any banks currently? 1 = no, 2 = somewhat, 3 = yes, very good			
6. How much experience do you have in this field? 1 = 0-1 year, 2 = 2-4 years, 3 = 5 years or more			
Total			

Now take the total from column 1 and multiply it by 1 = _____

Now take the total from column 2 and multiply it by 2 = _____

Now take the total from column 3 and multiply it by 3 = _____

Now add that total up and put it here   = _____

If that total is between

6 – 8 = You should consider bootstrapping your company and having an alternative income until your business becomes profitable. You are considered a high risk investment for any financial institution therefore you will need to prove that your business is profitable.

9 – 11 = You could qualify for some loans and you should explore these options. You are not a high risk but you are not an easy risk either. You would need to have good experience and a good business plan in order to get funding.

12 – 15 = You are a pretty good investment and could obtain a loan or funding from investors based on the feasibility of your business plan.

16 – 18 = You are a sound investment and you can easily obtain funding from investors or a loan if your business plan is solid.

Copyright

What is copyright?
Copyright is a form of protection grounded in the U.S. Constitution and granted by law for original works of authorship fixed in a tangible medium of expression. Copyright covers both published and unpublished works.

What does copyright protect?
Copyright, a form of intellectual property law, protects original works of authorship including literary, dramatic, musical, and artistic works such as poetry, novels, movies, songs, computer software and architecture. Copyright does not protect facts, ideas, systems or methods of operation, although it may protect the way these things are expressed.

How is a copyright different from a patent or a trademark?
Copyright protects original works of authorship, while a patent protects inventions or discoveries. Ideas and discoveries are not protected by the copyright law, although the way in which they are expressed may be. A trademark protects words, phrases, symbols or designs identifying the source of the goods or services of one party and distinguishing them from those of others.

When is my work protected?
Your work is under copyright protection the moment it is created and fixed in a tangible form that it is perceptible either directly or with the aid of a machine or device.

Do I have to register with the copyright office to be protected?
No. In general, registration is voluntary. Copyright exists from the moment the work is created. You will have to register, however, if you wish to bring a lawsuit for infringement of a U.S. work.

Why should I register my work if copyright protection is automatic?
Registration is recommended for a number of reasons. Many choose to register their works because they wish to have the facts of their copyright on the public record and have a certificate of registration. Registered works may be eligible for statutory damages and attorney's fees in successful litigation. Finally, if registration occurs within 5 years of publication, it is considered *prima facie* evidence in a court of law.

I've heard about a "poor man's copyright." What is it?
The practice of sending a copy of your own work to yourself is sometimes called a "poor man's copyright." There is no provision in the copyright law regarding any such type of protection, and it is not a substitute for registration.

Is my copyright good in other countries?
The United States has copyright relations with most countries throughout the world, and as a result of these agreements, we honor each other's citizens' copyrights. However, the United States does not have such copyright relationships with every country.

Can I copyright my Website?
The original authorship appearing on a website may be protected by copyright. This includes writings, artwork, photographs and other forms of authorship protected by copyright.

Which form should I use?
Generally, to register literary works and computer programs, use Form TX; for performing arts, use Form PA; for single issue serials/periodicals, use Form SE; for a group of issues of serials/periodicals, use Form SE/Group; for a group of daily newspapers or newsletters, use Form G/DN; for sound recordings, use Form SR; for visual arts, use Form VA.

What is the difference between Form PA and Form SR?
These forms are for registering two different types of copyrightable works that may be embodied in a recording. Form PA is used for the registration of music and/or lyrics (as well as other works of the performing arts), even if your song is on a cassette. Form SR is used for registering the performance and production of a particular recording of sounds.

I want to copyright my business name. Which form do I use?
Names, titles, short phrases, and slogans are not copyrightable. You may have protection under the federal trademark laws. Contact the U.S. Patent & Trademark Office, 800-786-9199, for more information.

Which form do I use to register an automated database?
Use Form TX to register the copyright for a database.

Which form do I use to register a computer software application I am creating?
You should file your claim on application Form TX.

What is the registration fee?
The current filing fee is $30 per application. Generally, each work requires a separate application.

What are you trying to copyright?

_____

_____

_____

What form would be best for you?

_____

All forms are located at: http://www.copyright.gov/forms/

*information obtained from http://www.copyright.gov

Trademarks and Servicemarks

Trademark – A word, phrase, slogan, design or symbol used to identify goods and distinguish them from competitive products.

Servicemark – Marks used in the sale or advertising of services to identify and distinguish the services of one company from those of others.

What form do I use to register a trademark/service mark?
The Illinois Trademark or Service Mark Application. With this application you need three (3) images of your trademark/service mark that are 3" x 3". You also need to declare on your application your industry and business category. This form can be obtained from the Illinois business website located at:
http://www.cyberdriveillinois.com/departments/business_services/publications_and_forms/home.html

What is the cost to register a trademark in Illinois and California?
The cost is $10 in IL, $70 in CA

What is the cost to register a federal trademark?
The cost is $330.

What is the difference between a state and federal trademark/service mark?
A state trademark registration allows a registrant to enforce his rights against all subsequent users of the name within the state, while a federal trademark is effective throughout the 50 United States. It is recommended that a federal trademark registration be filed if there are sales conducted across state lines or outside the United States.

Does your business provide a service or product?   ☐Service   ☐Product

Would you need a trademark or servicemark?   ☐Trademark ☐Servicemark

Do you have three images of your trademark/servicemark?   ☐Yes ☐No

If No, how soon could you get three (3) images?
_____

_____

_____

Part III
Business Plan Template

Very few people have goals so clear that they have written them down. How can you get to "*success*" if you don't have a plan.
- J. Success -

Executive Summary (1 page)
Mission and Vision (one paragraph about the mission of your business)

_____

_____

_____

Opportunity (one paragraph about what needs or wants your business will fulfill)

_____

_____

_____

Market Strategy (one paragraph about the markets you will focus on and how you will reach those markets)

_____

_____

_____

Business Strategy (one paragraph about how your business will function)

_____

_____

_____

Financial Projections (3 year annual outlook of your business)

	Year 1	Year 2	Year 3
Revenues			
Net Profits			
Net Margin (%)			

Company History (one - two paragraphs on the history of your company, who started the company, what are their qualifications and education, when was the company started and why was the company started)

_____

_____

_____

_____

Business Concept

Description of Business (one – two pages detailing your entire business and what it does)

_____

_____

_____

_____

_____

_____

_____

_____

_____

_____

_____

_____

_____

Business Model (one – two pages of how your business will make money, how much will be profit, how much of the market you intend to obtain and what is your growth projection. Here you can also use charts and graphs that show your market share, profit, revenue and growth)

_____

_____

_____

_____

_____

_____

_____

_____

_____

_____

_____

	Year 1	Year 2	Year 3
Gross Revenue			

	Year 1	Year 2	Year 3
Operating Costs			

	Year 1	Year 2	Year 3
Net Profit			

	Year 1	Year 2	Year 3
Net Margin			

Goals and Objectives (list of short and long term goals for your business – list them all)

<u>Long Term Goals</u> (goals for the next 1 – 3 years)

1. _____
2. _____
3. _____
4. _____
5. _____
6. _____
7. _____

<u>Short Term Goals</u> (goals for the next week to month)

1. _____
2. _____
3. _____
4. _____
5. _____
6. _____
7. _____

<u>Keys to Success</u> (things that the business needs to accomplish to become successful)

1. _____
2. _____
3. _____
4. _____
5. _____
6. _____
7. _____

Industry Overview (one page overview of your industry, recent changes and outlook of the industry)

_____

_____

_____

_____

_____

_____

_____

_____

_____

_____

_____

_____

_____

_____

_____

_____

_____

_____

_____

_____

Business Organization

<u>Management</u> (paragraph for each individual that is in charge of the company) Describe their qualifications and accomplishments as well as what their responsibilities will be.

Name 1: _____

      Title:_____

Background and Qualifications:

_____

_____

_____

Job Description:

_____

_____

_____

_____

Name 2:_____

      Title:_____

Background and Qualifications:

_____

_____

_____

Job Description:

_____

_____

_____

_____

_____

<u>Organizational Chart</u> (this chart shows the company structure)

<u>Year One</u>

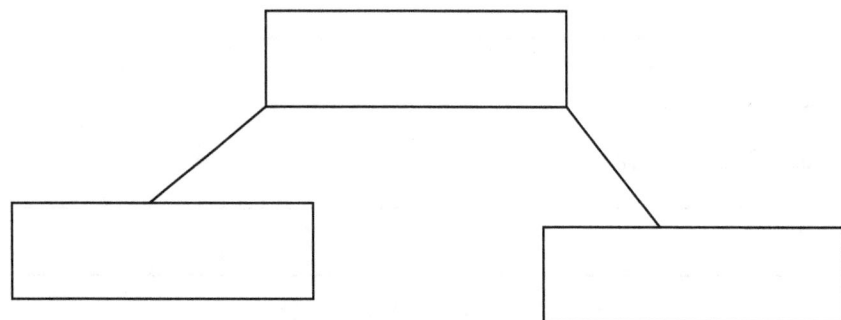

<u>Year Two</u>

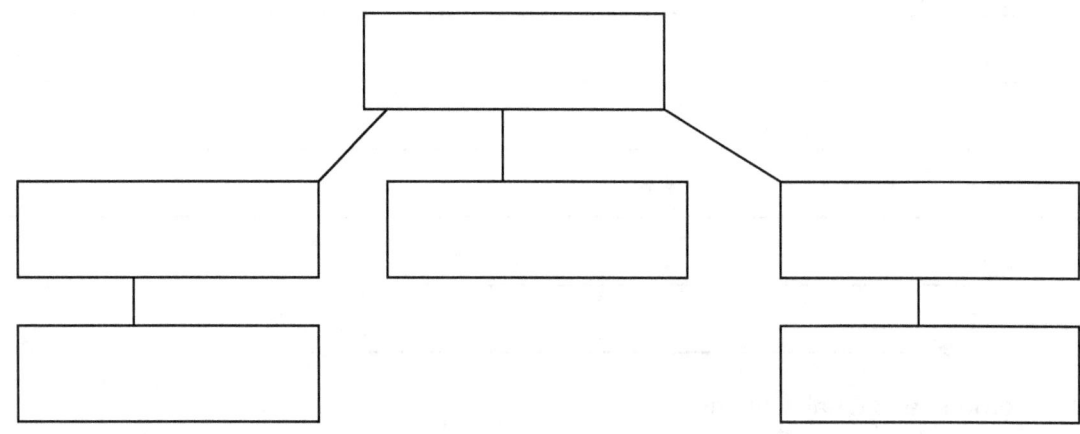

Core Competencies (These are the benefits and highlights of your company, these facts are what would make someone desire to do business with you).

> ➤ _____

> _____

> ➤ _____

> _____

> ➤ _____

> _____

> ➤ _____

> _____

> ➤ _____

> _____

Challenges (These are the challenges that your business might face while trying to achieve success).

> ➤ _____

> _____

> ➤ _____

> _____

> ➤ _____

> _____

> ➤ _____

> _____

> ➤ _____

> _____

Marketing Plan
Product (define what you offer in general terms)

_____

_____

_____

_____

Positioning (describe your product's unique features that make it different from other products)

_____

_____

_____

_____

Pricing (describe what will you products/services will cost and why)

_____

_____

_____

_____

Packaging (if you sell retail then explain how you will package your product to get people to notice it)

_____

_____

_____

_____

<u>Sales and Distribution</u>
Targeted Channels (who will buy your product or services, be specific)

_____

_____

_____

_____

Sales Strategy (who will sell your services and how will your services be sold)

_____

_____

_____

_____

<u>Marketing Strategy</u>
Advertising and Promotion (what will you do to advertise and get the word out about your product)

_____

_____

_____

_____

What advertising tools will you use most often?

☐ Promotion (sales, coupons, discounts)	☐ Trade shows
☐ Public relations (publicist)	☐ Catalogs
☐ Website	☐ Direct mailings (postcards)
☐ E-mail	☐ Flyers
☐ Newsletters	☐ Brochures
☐ Word of Mouth	☐ Newspapers, magazines
☐ Other	☐ Other

Competitive Analysis (what do your competitors offer and how can you overcome them)

_____

_____

_____

_____

Financial Plan

Financial Request (one paragraph detailing how much money you need to get this venture started. Also detail why your company is worth receiving this money)

_____

_____

_____

_____

_____

Startup Costs (detailed list showing the costs of everything you need in order to start you business...do not leave anything out, make sure you focus on all that your business needs to have a successful start).

Accounting $_____

Legal $_____

Advertising $_____

Licenses $_____

Rent $_____

Salaries $_____

Supplies $_____

Utilities/Phone $_____

Miscellaneous $_____

_____ $_____

_____ $_____

_____ $_____

Total $_____

<u>Personal Financial Statement</u> (This is a picture of your net worth right now. You will fill in your assets and liabilities)

Assets:
Cash: $_____
Savings Accounts $_____
IRA or Retirement $_____
Life Insurance $_____
Stocks and Bonds $_____
Real Estate $_____
Automobile $_____
Other Property $_____
Other Assets $_____

Total Assets $_____

Liabilities
Accounts Payable $_____
Auto Loan $_____
Mortgages $_____
Unpaid Taxes $_____
Other Liabilities $_____

Total Liabilities $_____

Income:
Salary $_____
Investments $_____
Real Estate $_____
Other $_____

Total Income $_____

Net Worth = (Assets + Income) – Liabilities = _____

Break Even Analysis

Break-even analysis focuses on the relationship between fixed cost, variable cost, and profit. Businesses need to know how many units they need to sell to cover costs and where they begin to make a profit.

# of Months	_____	
Projected Sales	$_____	
Variable Costs		
Materials	$_____	
Labor	$_____	
Other	$_____	
Total Variable Costs	$_____	
Fixed Costs		
Accounting	$_____	
Legal	$_____	
Advertising	$_____	
Licenses	$_____	
Rent	$_____	
Salaries	$_____	
Supplies	$_____	
Utilities/Phone	$_____	
Miscellaneous	$_____	
Total Fixed Costs	$_____	
Total Costs	$_____	(Variable Costs + Fixed Costs)
Break Even Point	$_____	Point which (Revenue = Total Costs)
Monthly Break Even	$_____	(Break Even Point/ 12)
Profit	$_____	(Revenue – Total Costs)

<u>Annual Income for 3 years</u>

	Year 1	Year 2	Year 3	Totals
Sales				
Labor				
Materials				
Wages				
Taxes (usually 15% up to 50K)				
Rent				
Utilities				
Insurance				
Payroll				
Supplies				
Advertising				
Marketing				
Professional Fees				
Miscellaneous				
Total Expenses				
Sales – Expenses				
Cumulative Income (Year 2 = year 1 income + year 2) (Year 3 = year 2 income + year 3)				

Conclusion (one paragraph summary of the entire business plan and why this business will be successful).

_____

_____

_____

_____

_____

_____

_____

*Always Be Prepared – If this venture does not work out, what is your alternative plan?

_____

_____

_____

_____

_____

Glossary

Accelerated Depreciation-Any depreciation method that produces depreciation at a greater rate in the early years of an asset's life.

Account-A record of all the debits and credits chronologically posted to a ledger showing how each transaction affects a particular phase of a business. Entries are usually stated in monetary figures and reflect the current balances, if any.

Accountant-A person engaged in accounting work.

Accounting-The process of identifying, measuring, recording and communicating financial information about a business or organization. Accounting information can be a helpful aid in the decision making process.

Accounts Payable-Money owed by a person or company. Carried in the current liabilities section of the firm's balance sheet.

Accounts Receivable-Money due from customers carried as "open book" accounts. Carried in the current assets section of the firm's balance sheet.

Accrual-Basis Accounting-An accounting system in which income and expenses are recorded when an obligation is made rather than when money is received or paid.

Accrue-To periodically grow or accumulate.

Accrued Interest-Interest that has been earned but has not yet been paid.

Administration-A group of people who make the management decisions in an organization.

Advisory Board-A group of individuals willing to serve in an advisory capacity in exchange for stock or other benefits.

Aging Of Receivables- (1) an inventory of accounts receivable classified by the debt's age; (2) a method of estimating bad-debt losses by aging the accounts and then assigning a probability of collection to each classification. For example, accounts aged more than six months might be assumed to be worthless, while those more than 90 days delinquent might be assumed to be worth only 50 cents on the dollar.

Agreement-A mutual understanding between two or more parties. This may or may not constitute a contract.

Amortization- (1) The process of liquidating a debt through installment payments. (2) Prorating expenditures over time in order to write them off.

Amortize-The gradual reduction of a debt by making periodic payments until the total has been satisfied.

Anchor Store-A large, well-known store in a shopping mall; considered by developers and merchants to be an attraction to draw customers. The presence of such an anchor increases the market potential for other businesses and makes adjacent locations more desirable for entrepreneurs. Malls without powerful anchor stores encounter financial difficulty.

Angel-A private investor who often has non-monetary motives for investing as well as the usual financial ones.

Angel Capital-Start-up money provided to entrepreneurs by friends, family or wealthy individuals whose motives may be non-monetary as well as financial.

Annual Net Profits Or Losses-The balance of the business' proceeds at the end of every year after all direct, operating, interest and tax expenses are paid.

Annual Percentage Rate (APR)-An interest rate that states the true cost of obtaining credit for the duration of the loan.

Annual Report-A detailed document prepared by a company at the end of its reporting year. This report usually contains various financial reports, information on company officers and directors, as well as an analysis on past and future operations of the company.

Armchair Entrepreneur-A person who loves to talk about new ventures and what he/she plans to do about them, but never does anything; he/she is all talk and no action.

Asset-An item that has value and is owned by an individual or corporation.

Asset Lending-The loaning of money on the value of assets offered as security. The lender is protected from loss by the liquidation value of the assets.

Assumptions-Preconceived notices or hunches on which management bases reasonable financial projections or other probable developments. Usually found in the financial section of the corporate business plan.

Audit-To examine an individual's or organization's records in an attempt to verify accuracy and legal compliance.

Auditor-A person who is qualified to examine and verify accounts.

Back order-Part of an order that was not filled when the initial shipment was made. Back orders are usually shipped when the items become available without the customer having to place a reorder.

Backup-To duplicate an item in the event the original is damaged or destroyed.

Backup System-Standby or alternate components in a computer processing system that can be used in case of loss or damage to the primary component.

Bad Credit-The result of a company or individual being late or defaulting on bill payment.

Bad Debt-Money that is still owed on an account and is past due.

Balance Sheet-An accounting statement showing the financial condition of a company at a point in time; presents assets, liabilities, and net worth. Basic equation: assets=liabilities+ net worth.

Bank Statement-A printed statement of a customer's account regularly provided by the bank.

Bankrupt-A person or business that is unable to meet its financial obligations, and a court decree has declared the person or business insolvent. The person or business comes under the administration of the bankruptcy laws for the benefit of the creditors.

Bankruptcy-A voluntary or involuntary state in which one is unable to meet financial obligations as they become due and a court has so declared.

Barter-The exchange of one commodity for another without the exchange of money.

Barter Arrangement-An agreement to exchange goods or services directly without money as a medium of exchange. A great tool for the entrepreneur.

Belly Up-Comparison of the death of a venture to that of a goldfish; going bankrupt.

Better Business Bureau (BBB)-A not –for-profit association of local businesses that attempts to control unethical business practices. Consumers information is available through the association.

Big Ticket Item-Merchandise that is large in size and fairly expensive, i.e. car.

Bill Of Lading-Written document, a receipt, given by a transportation company, showing the name of the shipper and the receiver and itemizing the goods shipped.

Bill Of Sale-A written agreement stating the terms by which ownership of goods is transferred another party.

Blue Sky-Claims referring to future business profits that are greatly exaggerated or even nonexistent.

Blue-Collar Worker-A term referring to a class of wage earners whose duties are centered towards production and maintenance.

Board Of Advisors-A group of outside experts, typically three or six, recruited by entrepreneurs to provide regular input and suggestions to management. Many small companies use an advisory board in place of a board of directors, so as to avoid liability issues.

Bond-A form of interest-bearing note used by corporations to borrow on a long-term basis.

Bonus-Incentives given to employees in addition to base compensation. Can be in the form of cash award or a non-monetary form (gifts, extra vacation time, etc.).

Book Inventory-The balance of the inventory account after all incoming inventory is added and the cost of outgoing goods is subtracted. This type of perpetual inventory system is usually verified annually by taking a physical inventory and reconciling any discrepancies.

Book Value-The value of an asset as reflected in the books of the company owning the item.

Bookkeeper-A person who records the accounts or transactions of a business in a general ledger.

Boutique-A small shop or company that specializes in a particular business or offers limited services.

Boycott-An agreement between two or more parties not to do business with a third party. A boycott usually takes the form of a union and its members applying pressure on an employer to change some business practice.

Brainstorming-A management technique used to foster ideas, solve problems, set goals, establish priorities, and make assignments for their accomplishments.

Brand-A mark or symbol placed on an item or a group of products to differentiate them from competitors' products.

Breach Of Contract- (1) The breaking of a promise made to fulfill an obligation; (2) A violation of one's duty to carry out a contractual responsibility.

Break-Even Analysis-A means of determining the quantity that has to be sold at a given price so that revenues will equal cost. Break-even point in units=total fixed cost/ (unit price-unit variable cost).

Break-Even Point-The level of sales at which total revenue equals total costs incurred; the point at which the venture is meeting expenses with no profit, no loss.

Break-Even Pricing-Establishing a level of pricing that will enable a company to break even.

Bridge Loan-Short-term, temporary financing used permanent financing can be secured.

Bulk-Large quantities. Companies usually buy in bulk to realize a cost savings.

Bulk Discount-A reduction in the amount charged when purchases are made in large quantities or multiple purchases.

Business Ethics-The moral obligation placed on business leaders in a community to be honest and fair in their dealings with customers.

Business License- A permit or certification that local and state governments require businesses to obtain and post. Obtaining a license may merely require the payment of a fee to do business; in other cases, the proprietor may have to pass a test that certifies he or she is competent to perform certain services. Some licenses limit the number of businesses that can provide certain goods or services.

Business Philosophy-The unique outlook an entrepreneur, owner, or manager takes towards the conduct of business. Business philosophy determines, for example, the extent to which customer service takes precedence over hitting profit targets, whether employees are encouraged to take initiative or not, whether innovation is encouraged or resented. Entrepreneurs can share many business practices, for example accounting and financial systems, marketing strategies and the like, and yet differ considerably in their business or management philosophy.

Business Plan-A well researched and ever-changing document that provides direction and focus for both the day-to-day operations and the future growth of the business. A good business plan will include components covering management, the product and/or service, a marketing plan, financials, operations and control systems, and a growth plan and exit strategy.

Buyout Agreements- (1) A means of protecting principal parties in a venture from undue financial loss should the personal and/or business relationships among the founders or investors for some reason disintegrate, often including in buy-sell agreements. Saves aggravation, legal expense, goodwill of involved parties; (2) a wise provision inserted into agreements between private investors and entrepreneurs that allows them to get rid of troublesome investors.

Buy-Sell Agreements-Contracts between associates that set the terms and conditions by which one or more of the associates can buy out one or more of the other associates.

Bylaws-Rules under which a corporation is governed. These rules can be amended as provided by state law and the bylaws. Rules and regulations under which a board of directors operates a corporation.

By-Product-A secondary product that is produced in addition to the primary product.

C Corporation-A business organization in which the owners are taxed separately from the business.

C.O.D. (Cash On Delivery)-A term applied to any purchases that need to be paid for when delivered.

Cancellation Fee-A fee imposed for breaking a service contract.

Capital-A term commonly used as a synonym for cash. Capital Goods: material assets, equipment, machinery or tools, Capital Funds: cash assets.

Capital Assets-Items purchased for internal use rather than resale.

Capital Expenditure-Money spent for the purchase or expansion of plant or equipment.

Capital Gains-Short or long-term profits from that sale of assets.

Capital Investments-A term applied to investment capital used to purchase capital items like manufacturing equipment and real estate.

Carry Charge-Premium rates charged on overdue accounts.

Carrying Cost-Cost incurred from storage of inventory.

Cash and Carry-The terms of sale when the buyer must pay cash when he picks up the merchandise. Credit terms are not accepted and delivery services are usually not available.

Cash Basis Accounting-An accounting method that immediately records the receipt of cash or the expense for goods and services. This is not an accepted method of bookkeeping for publicly held companies.

Cash Cow-A product or service that sells very well and has a low cost. The name implies the relative ease with which cash is obtained-like milking a cow.

Cash Discount-A discount given to the buyer as an incentive to render immediate payment or payment within a specific time frame.

Cash Flow-The most important consideration of business survival. The measurement of the differences between the actual cash received by a firm and its actual cash expenditures. Only the flow of cash is measured. Non-cash transactions such as depreciation, amortization, credit sales and purchases on account are ignored.

Cash-Flow Projection-A forecast of the cash flow for a period of time in the future. Sometimes called a cash budget.

Central Buying-A buying approach whereby all purchasing of goods is done through a main or central office. Shipment of ordered goods is usually made directly to the store for which it was ordered, or through a distribution center that repackages the order for the individual stores.

Certificate Of Deposit-A certificate providing evidence that a bank has received funds deposited for a specific period of time.

Certificate Of Title-A certification given by a title company or attorney verifying the validity of a title.

Certified Check-A check guaranteed to be good by the bank on which it is drawn. In order to eliminate the risk of covering the check, many banks charge the depositor's account immediately for the amount of the check.

Certified Public Accountant (CPA)-An accountant who has met all of a state's requirements and has received a state certificate.

Channels Of Distribution-Systems of economic institutions through which goods flow into the hands of consumers or industrial firms.

Chief Executive Officer (CEO)-The top managerial position in a company.

Chief Financial Officer (CFO)-A member of a company's upper management who oversees all the financial aspects of the business.

Chief Operating Officer (COO)-An executive who oversees the daily operations of a company.

Close-To bring to an end; to finalize a sale or agreement.

Close Out-To liquidate or dispose of an entire inventory of goods usually by reducing prices below their previous retail price. Most businesses will do this when going out of business.

Closely Held Corporation-A corporation owned by a few individuals, who also own all the stock. No stock in the corporation is publicly traded. State regulations administer the establishment of corporations.

Closing Entries-An entry made in a ledger to bring a temporary account to a zero balance in preparation for the next accounting period.

Cold Call-An unscheduled call or visit by a seller to a potential buyer.

Collateral-The asset(s), such as real property or an automobile, which is offered as security for a loan.

Commerce-The buying and selling of commodities between states and nations.

Commercial Bank-State or nationally chartered bank that accepts demands deposits, grants business loans and provides a variety of other financial services. Typically used by the entrepreneur as an asset lender.

Commission-An incentive fee paid to salesperson to reward them for the amount of business they generate. The commission rate is usually figured at a fixed rate or a percentage of sales.

Committee-A group of persons who meet regularly to consider, deliberate or make a decision on some matter.

Common Law-Law that results from judicial decisions or custom without the aid of written legislation.

Common Stock-Shares that represent the ownership interest in a corporation. Both common and preferred stock have ownership rights, but the preferred normally has prior claim on dividends and, in the event of liquidation, assets. Both common and preferred stockholders' claims are junior to claims of bondholders or other creditors of the company. Common stockholders assume the greater risk, but have the voting power and generally exercise the greater control and may gain the greater reward in the form of dividends and capital appreciation. Common stock and capital stock are terms often used interchangeably when the company has no preferred stock.

Company-An association of people organized for purposes of carrying on a commercial or industrial enterprise.

Compensation-Rewards given to employees based on their contributions or the value of their jobs. These rewards can be monetary or non-monetary.

Competition- (1) Any rivalry between two competitors; (2) When two or more parties acting independently try to secure the business of a third party by offering the best terms available.

Competitive Edge-The factors that give a company an advantage over its competitors in the marketplace. One theory of entrepreneurship is that the venture must develop some competitive edge if it is to profitably exist in the market.

Competitive Pricing-A price established by a number of buyers and sellers negotiating independently in a market setting.

Concept- (1) A set of thoughts that communicate to others the precise nature of the enterprise one proposing to undertake; (2) A set of cohesive ideas about how to create and deliver value to a market.

Consignee-The person who receives shipped or consigned goods.

Consignment-A policy of placing one's goods with a middleman or prospective customer, while retaining title to them. The middleman or customer does not pay for the goods until they are sold or used. If they remain unsold, the goods may be returned.

Consignor-A person who delivers or addresses goods to an agent to be cared for or sold.

Consultant-An individual who provides advice, counsel, feedback, and sometimes implementation services on any of a variety of management issues ranging from strategic planning to marketing to financing to production.

Consumer-Any person who uses or consumes economic goods and services.

Consumer Behavior-The activities of individuals in the marketplace including the process involved in decision-making, purchasing and evaluation; how people go about acquiring their standard of living.

Consumer Goods-The items that a consumer purchases for personal or household consumption.

Consumer Price Index (CPI)-A measure of inflation used in the United States, calculated by the U.S. Bureau of Labor Statistics.

Contract-A promise or a set of promises for the breach of which the law gives a remedy or the performance of which the law in some way recognizes as a duty.

Contract Labor-Workers hired on an "as needed basis" to do specific work.

Contracting Out-Allowing subcontractors to perform part of a job rather than one company's employees performing the entire task.

Convenience Goods-Goods that consumers want to buy with a minimum effort; usually relatively low-priced items that are purchased frequently.

Cooperative Advertising-Advertising that is paid for by both the retailers or wholesalers and the advertiser.

Copyright-An exclusive right granted by the federal government to the creator to publish and sell literary, musical and other artistic materials. Honored for 50 years after the death of the creator.

Corporate Bylaws-Specific rules concerning the internal affairs of a corporation.

Corporate Licensing-Using popular corporate names to sell products with which they have not been previously associated.

Corporate Tax-A tax assessed by states on their resident corporations. Levy terms and percentages vary widely from state to state.

Corporation-A legal entity created under state law. A form of organization wherein ownership is vested in the stockholders. Chief Justice John Marshall's classic definition (1819) reads: A corporation is an official being, invisible, intangible, and existing in contemplation of law. Being the mere creature of law, it possesses only those properties, which the charter of its creation confers upon it, either expressly, or as incidental to its very existence. These are such as the same, and may act as a single individual. They enable a corporation to manage its own affairs, and to hold property without the perplexing intricacies, the hazardous and endless necessity, of perpetual conveyances for the purpose of transmitting it from hand to hand. It is chiefly for the purpose of clothing bodies of men, in succession, with these qualities and capacities, that corporations were invested, and are in use. By these means, a perpetual succession of individuals is capable of acting for the promotion of the particular object, like an immortal being [Dartmouth College v. Woodward 4 Wheaton (U.S.) 518 (1819)].

Cost Of Goods Sold- (1) Purchase price of merchandise sold by a retailer; (2) the cost of raw materials, purchased part and labor in making a product; (3) that which is deducted from net sales to determine gross margin (gross profit).

Creator-The innovator, the one who conceives and nurtures the idea. Someone with creativity, intuition, and perception, possibly a right-brain thinker.

Credit- (1) An entry on the right-hand side of an account ledger representing an addition to a revenue or liability account. (2) The ability to borrow a sum of money or purchase an item with the understanding that the balance will be repaid at a later date.

Credit Card-A card issued by a business that entitles the holder to purchase items on credit at participating retailers.

Credit Report-A confidential report that is usually generated as a result of a credit investigation into an applicant's background. It details the financial standings of an applicant.

Creditor-Individuals or firms to which money is owed. (1) General: class of claimants who are paid from funds remaining after preferred and security creditors have been satisfied; they have no preferred status or security for their claims. (2) Preferred: class of claims that must be paid first, by order of court in bankruptcy cases, including: taxes, wages, court costs, secured creditors.

Current Assets-Cash or property that can be converted to cash in a short period of time; usually accounts receivable, inventory and short-term notes receivable.

Current Liability-A debt, which is payable within one year or within the normal operating cycle of a company; usually accounts payable, accrued expenses payable and short-term notes payable.

Current Ratio-A ratio that indicates a firm's degree of liquidity by dividing current assets by current liabilities.

Customer-An individual, business, or other organization that purchases a good or service from a business entity.

Customer-In-Hand-Customer already interested enough and ready to purchase a product or service-advance orders, deposits.

Damages-Monetary loss experienced by a party as a result of a wrongful act or negligence.

Data Processing-The conversion of crude information into usable or storable data.

Database-An integrated collection of data stored in different record types.

Dealer-An individual or company that sells or distributes goods or services to a customer.

Debit-An entry in the left side of an account ledger representing an addition to an asset or expense account.

Debt-Something owed, such as money or services, to another person.

Debt Capital-Funds or assets acquired by borrowing.

Debt Service-The money needed to pay the amount due on a loan.

Debt-To-Assets Ratio-The relationship of a company's total debt to its total assets. The lower the ratio, the more financially sound a company is thought to be.

Debt-To-Equity Ratio-The relationship of debt to stockholder equity (ownership), or net worth, in a firm's capital structure. The higher the ratio, i.e., the more debt there is relative to equity, the greater the firm is leveraged.

Deduction-An item that can be subtracted from income to determine one's taxable income.

Default-Failure to pay a debt, make scheduled payments, or meet any term of a credit contract.

Delinquency-A past-due credit account or debt payment.

Demographics-The science of grouping human populations statistically by such characteristics as age, sex, family size, income, and occupation.

Depreciation-The periodic allocation of the cost of a tangible long-lived asset over its estimated useful life, man-made assets only. An exception is land which has unlimited life, therefore land is not subject to depreciation; natural-resources depletion.

Direct Cost-Any expense that a company incurs from the inception phase of a product or service to the distribution phase, such as raw materials, transportation costs and labor used to manufacture the product.

Direct Mail-Presenting a product or service to the consumer without the use of middlemen. This allows control over distribution and measures effectiveness of promotional campaigns.

Direct Mail List-A list that has been given to or purchased by an organization that contains the names and addresses of potential customers.

Direct Marketing-A term typically used to describe marketing that uses mailings-such as catalogs or third-class mail pieces. The advantage of direct marketing is that the results can be precisely measured.

Disbursement-The act of paying out funds to satisfy a financial obligation.

Discretionary Income-Amount of disposable personal income available for spending and saving after the basic necessities of food, clothing, and shelter has been provided.

Distribution Channel-The various organizations responsible for moving the product from the producer to the ultimate consumer.

Dividend-A distribution of profit made to the stockholders of a corporation. (1) Cash: payment in cash. (2) Extra: paid in either stock or cash in addition to the regular or usual dividend the corporation has been paying. (3) Property: payment in assets other than cash-inventory, marketable securities of other companies, fixed assets, etc. (4) Stock: payment of dividend stock.

Double Taxation-A term referring to the fact that earnings of a corporation may be taxed twice, both as the net income of the corporation and again as the dividends distributed to the stockholders. Adept management can often abate its impact in closed corporations.

Down Payment-A partial payment of the full price, made at the time of purchase or delivery, with the balance to be paid at a future date.

Driving Force-Someone with the energy and vision to take a business concept and make it a reality: the organizer in small-scale operations; the CEO in larger operations.

Dun & Bradstreet-A firm that gathers and sells credit information on business firms.

Earnings-Total remuneration of an employee or group of employees for work performed, including wages, bonuses, commissions, etc.

E-Commerce-Business transactions facilitated by electronic technology, including private telephone and cable lines, Internet Websites and e-mail, and corporate intranets. It can include using computers to place orders with suppliers, invoice and bill customers, and ship goods, among other functions.

Eighty/Twenty Principle-A phenomenon in which a venture may get 80 percent of its business from 20 percent of its product line, while spending 80 percent of its effort to gain the remaining 20 percent of volume.

Employee-An individual who works for an employer in exchange for a wage or salary.

Employment Contract-An agreement between an employer and an individual to induce him or her to work for the company. The need for a contract arises when a firm wants a talented person to leave a good job to come work for it and that person demands assurances of fair treatment. Most managers are reluctant to offer these contracts.

Employment Taxes (Payroll Taxes)-Any variety of taxes levied by government, based on an employer's contributions to Social Security are known as FICA (Federal Insurance Contribution Act), also FUTA (Federal Unemployment Tax Act).

Entrepreneur-Derived from the French word "to undertake." Someone who is willing and eager to create a new venture in order to present a concept to the marketplace.

Entrepreneurship-A process through which individuals and groups pursue opportunity, leverage resources, and initiate change to create value. Thus, an entrepreneur is one who creates and manages change by pursuing opportunity, acting with passion for a purpose, living proactively, and leveraging resources to create value.

Entry Strategy-The way an entrepreneur plans to get business. Some of the various strategies are: Franchising, Buying a Business, Engaging in a Part-time Business, Expanding a Hobby, Spinning off from Current Employment, Observing of Market Need, Exploiting of Invention, Turnarounds, and Inventions.

Equity-Total assets minute total liabilities equals equity or net worth.

Equity Capital-Funds invested in a business by its owner(s).

Escrow-Placing money in a special and separate account under the control of another party, usually a financial institution, to be held until the completion of conditions set forth in an agreement.

Executive Summary-A document that captures and presents succinctly the essence of the written plan. It is, in effect, a capsulized version of the entire plan. The executive summary is not simply a background statement, nor is it an introduction. It is the plan in miniature. Because many plan reviewers are inundated with proposals, they use the executive summary for a quick understanding of the total plan.

Exit Strategy- (1) The way an entrepreneur gets his/her money out of the venture; (2) The vehicle for selling the enterprise; (3) What venture capitalists look for when funding new ventures-their way to realize the dollar profits from the investment.

Factoring- (1) The selling of accounts receivable; (2) Selling invoices at a discount.

Feasibility Plan-The process of determining the viability of a business concept by exploring the demand, size, and profitability of the proposed market, the availability of funding sources, and by making sure that the business and the personal criteria of the entrepreneur are a good match.

Feasibility Study-Research to determine the economic feasibility of a proposed business venture.

Fica (Federal Insurance Contributions Act)-A payroll deduction required by the federal government to help finance programs for retired Americans. It also provides disability benefits and health insurance for the aged.

FIFO (First In, First Out Method)-An inventory costing method under which the cost of the first items purchased are assigned to the items sold, and the cost of the inventory is composed of the cost of items from the first purchased.

Finance Charge-Total cost of credit in dollars and cents to obtain credit.

Financial Statement-Periodic accounting reports of a company's activities. Usually includes balance sheet and income statement.

Fiscal Year-A Corporation's accounting period that consists of twelve consecutive months.

Fixed Asset-Property with relatively long life, such as land, buildings and equipment.

Fixed Capital-Money invested in fixed assets.

Fixed Cost-A cost that remains constant within a relevant range of volume or activity.

FOB (Free On Board)-A delivery term indicating that the seller is responsible for the shipment of goods and the expense of shipment to the FOB point of designation. For example, if the terms of the shipment are "FOB shipping point," then the retail store must pay all expenses from the vendor's shipping point. However, when the

terms state "FOB store," then the vendor incurs all expenses until the merchandise reaches the store's receiving dock.

Focus Group-Structured discussion with a select, predetermined group of potential consumers to learn their reactions to a new product or service.

Franchise-A contract between two parties. In modern usage, it is a license from the franchiser that entitles its holder to operate a particular type of business according to certain stated conditions and arrangements.

Franchising-A distribution system by which a parent company is linked to independent companies that buy a right to own and operate the franchise along the lines of the parent company's comprehensive marketing program.

General Ledger-The primary record, when used in conjunction with subsidiary ledgers, that contains all of the balance sheet and income statement accounts.

General Partnership-An agreement in which all partners are completely liable for the indebtedness brought about by the partnership or any partner.

Going Public-A privately held company electing to sell a portion of its common shares of stock to the public. Also referred to as an initial public offering (IPO).

Goodwill-The difference between the market value of a firm and the market value of its net tangible assets.

Gross Margin-Net sales minus cost of goods sold; sometimes known as gross profit.

Gross Sales-Total sales for a given accounting period. Includes goods that are later returned.

Growth Potential-The difference between a venture's present sales volume and its sales potential.

Home-Based Business-Usually an entrepreneurial business operated from one's own home.

Import-To receive goods or services from one country into another.

Importer-One who buys goods from foreign markets.

Income Statement-A financial statement that shows the amount of income earned by a business over a specific accounting period. All costs (expenses) are subtracted from the gross revenues (sales) to determine net income, which outlines the profit-and-loss financial statement

(P&L).

Income Tax-A tax applied to the net income of an individual or a business.

Incorporate-To form a corporation according to the laws of the various states governing incorporation. Tax and other laws can vary depending on the type of corporation, of which there are the "C" corporation and the subchapter S corporation.

Incubator Space-A rental space for start-up businesses found on university campuses and industrial parks, often sponsored by city governments. Incubators nurture young companies by offering work space at low rent, business services at low cost, and opportunities for consultation with business experts.

Independent Audit-An audit conducted by an auditor who is not associated with the company whose books are being reviewed.

Independent Contractor-A person who is hired by a company to perform a specific job in a designated period of time. The worker is not recognized as an employee of the organization and is not entitled to the company benefits.

Indirect Cost-A manufacturing cost that is not traceable to a specific product or cost objective and which must be assigned by some allocation method.

Industries Overview-The history, participants, total sales volume, trends, growth potential, and other pertinent facts on a particular industry.

Inflation-An increase in the general price level resulting in a decline in the purchasing power of money.

Infrastructure-Specialists (outside the normal management team) such as attorneys, CPAs, bankers, insurance brokers, consultants, and other types of advisers who provide necessary support and resources to the entrepreneur to operate a business.

Insured And Bonded-Protection measures applied to employees, usually in the construction industry, to prevent owners and their customers from incurring damages because of injuries or thefts on the job.

Intangible Assets-Assets that have no physical substance although they can provide economic benefits to a company. Notable intangible assets are goodwill and copyrights.

Intellectual Property-Intangible property usually developed from the knowledge, ideas, and talent of individuals. For example, patents, trademarks and trade names, copyrights, trade secrets, customers and customer lists, and valuable employees. Generally, rights to intellectual property can be legally protected. However, pursuing such rights has been complicated by the cost of litigation and the impact of technology and global competition.

Interest-A charge for borrowing money.

Interest Rate-A percentage rate charged on the amount of money that is borrowed, usually stated as an annual percentage rate (APR).

Internet Marketing-Using the Web and e-mail to deliver marketing messages to target audiences, building relationships with individuals in those audiences and/or providing customer support via post-sale interactions.

Inventory-The quantity of goods that are on hand available for use or resale.

Inventory Control-Process of balancing incoming and outgoing stock to assure that adequate supplies are on hand with which to do business.

Inventory Turnover-The ratio upon purchase of inventory; includes invoice price less cash discount plus freight and transportation and applicable insurance, taxes and tariffs.

Investment-The outlay of money for the purpose of making more money for either income or profit or both.

Invoice-itemized list of goods sent by seller to buyer. Usually gives prices, terms of sale, shipping dates or any other information relevant to the sale.

IPO (Initial Public Offering)-A company's first registration and sale of stock to the public. The reasons for an IPO are (1) to provide an opportunity for existing investors to turn a profit, since for the first time their shares will be given a market value reflection the expectations for the company's future growth, and (2) To potentially raise significant amounts of capital to fuel the planned and/or continued growth o f the privately held company.

IRS-Form W-4-A form employees complete and give to their employers to establish their filing status and the number of withholding allowances.

IRS (Internal Revenue Service)-Federal agency that interprets and enforces the U.S. tax laws governing the assessment and collection of revenue for operating the government.

ISP (Internet Service Provider)-Companies that supply Internet accounts and server space for Web pages.

Itemized Deductions-A list of allowed expenses that a taxpayer can deduct to arrive at her/his taxable income. These deductions include but are not limited to such items as contributions to charitable organizations, various health care expenses, qualified home mortgage interest and investment interest.

Joint Venture-Usually refers to a short-lived partnership with each partner sharing in costs and rewards of the project; common in research, investment banking, and the healthcare industry.

Lead-A potential customer who has not been contacted by a salesperson or company.

Lead Blocker-Someone or something that provides an easier entrance or acceptance into a target market, such as associated products, celebrity endorsements, or affiliation with a reputable person or institution.

Lease-A form of contract that conveys to another the right to possess property in return for payment, usually in the form of rent. In a lease, the person who conveys the property is the lessor and the person who holds the property under a lease is the lessee.

Lease Financing-Financing the acquisition of plant or equipment by leasing it rather than buying it.

Leasehold Improvement-An improvement to leased property, considered an intangible asset to the lessee that becomes the property of the lessor at the end of the lease.

Lease-Purchase Agreement-An agreement wherein part of the lessee's monthly rent is applied toward the purchase of the property. When the agreed equity is reached, the ownership is transferred to the lessee.

Legal Structure-The various forms of business organizational structure: Sole Proprietorship, Partnership, Corporation, S Corporation, Not-for-profit Corporation, Limited Liability Company.

Lender-An individual or financial institution that temporarily lends out money with the expectation that it will be repaid in full with interest.

Lessee-One who holds property under a lease.

Lessor-One who transfers property by lease, such as a landlord.

Letter of Credit-A bank's written guarantee of funds available for drafts written on it.

Letter of Intent-a letter addressed to a company from a customer, supplies, distributor, investor, or other interested party, stating the desire to conduct business. A letter of intent does not necessarily obligate the party writing it but can be an influential device to sway prospective investors or bankers to finance the venture based on evident industry and market support.

Liability-A debt of the business; an amount owed or an obligation to perform a service to creditors, employees, government bodies, or others; a claim against assets.

License-A document granting permission to engage in a business, occupation or activity that would otherwise be unlawful without the license.

Licensing Agreement-A legal contract in which the licensor grants to the licensee rights to use specific property, in return for which royalties will be paid.

Lien-A legal claim against property as security for repayment of a debt.

Lifestyle Firm-This term is often used to describe companies that place lifestyle issues-independence, location, hours, for example before expansion and growth as key priorities.

LIFO (Last-In, First-Out Method)-An inventory-costing method under which the cost of the last items purchased are assigned to the first items sold and the cost of the inventory is composed of the cost of items from the oldest purchases.

Limited Liability Company (LLC)-A type of business formation that allows the owners to be taxed as a partnership but with the limited liability of a corporation.

Limited Liability Partnership-A company organization that offers advantages of both partnership and incorporation, now available as an option in most states.

Limited Partner-An individual who has limited liability in a partnership. He/she cannot participate in management.

Line of Credit-Short-term financing usually granted by a bank up to a predetermined limit; debtor borrows as needed up to the limit of credit without need to renegotiate the loan.

Liquidation-The process of converting assets into cash.

Liquidity-The relative amount of ease in converting assets to cash.

List Broker-An organization or individual who prepares, organizes and rents mailing lists.

List Price-The price of an item recommended by the manufacturer. Also known as the suggested retail price, this is not necessarily the retail price at which the item sells after various discounts are taken.

Loan-An agreement between two parties in which the lender transfers an item to the borrower with the expectation of the item being returned at a later date. Many arrangements involve money being loaned with the repayment including interest as well as the principle loan.

Logo-An identifying graphic used by a company to represent itself or its products.

Long-Term Capital Gain-The gain achieved when selling capital assets that have been held for a period of twelve months or longer at a profit.

Long-Term Capital Loss-The deficit experienced when selling capital assets that have been held for a period of twelve months or longer at a loss.

Long-Term Debt-Loans that are to be paid back over a period greater than a year.

Long-Term Liabilities-Debt of a business that matures more than one year ahead, beyond the normal operating cycle or is to be paid out of non-current assets.

Loss Leader-A product/service priced below cost to attract customers to a retail business.

Management Team-A group of individuals who combine their talents to run an enterprise. These talents create a fully integrated system and often include: Driving Force, Creator/Innovator, Sales, Production, Engineering, Marketing, Finance.

Manager-A person who is responsible for overseeing the operation of a department or an organization. A manager also trains, directs and monitors employees to make sure department and company objectives are being met.

Manufacturer-A business engaged in the production of goods.

Manufacturer's Agent Or Manufacturer's Representative-An agent who generally operates on an extended contractual basis; often sells within an exclusive territory; handles non-competing but related lines of goods; and possesses limited authority with regard to prices and or sale terms.

Margin-Also called markup; the amount the entrepreneur adds to a product's cost to obtain its selling price.

Markdown-Reduction in price (usually in connection with retail pricing).

Market- (1) The actual and/or potential buyers of a product or service; (2) A place where exchanges between buyers and sellers occur.

Market Driven-An enterprise created to exploit a market opportunity.

Market Niche-A particular appeal, identity, or place in the market that your product/company has. What you do well, differently, or better than others in the market.

Market Penetration-The degree of success and acceptance of a product by a specified target market.

Market Positioning-The projection of a product as having a certain desired image that makes it appealing to a certain segment of the market for that type of product.

Market Price-The price for which a product can be sold in the market to a bona fide buyer.

Market Segment-A specified, homogeneous, identifiable portion of the market.

Market Share-That portion of the total market sold by a specific company, expressed as a percentage.

Marketing-The performance of business activities that direct the flow of goods and services from producer to consumer or user.

Marketing Plan-A written formulation for achieving the marketing goals and strategies of the venture, usually on an annual basis. Business plans always contain a marketing plan section.

Marketing Research-The systematic gathering, recording and analyzing of data about problems relating to the marketing of goods and services. Such research may be undertaken by impartial agencies or by business firms or their consultants for the solution to their marketing problems.

Markup-Amount added to the cost of a product/service to determine its retail price.

Mass Production-The production of standardized items in large quantities usually involving machinery.

Merchandising-A term that is used in many ways, depending upon the industry. (1) In retailing, it refers to all activities connected with buying and selling merchandise, including store display, promotional, pricing, and buying acumen. Even such factors as store layout and fixture design play a role in "merchandising a store." (2) In manufacturing, the term refers to the activities that are intended to make the offering attractive to potential buyers, such as packaging, sales promotion, special pricing deals, and other such promotional activities.

Merchant-A business unit that buys, takes title to, and resells merchandise.

Merchant Wholesaler-Wholesaler who takes title to goods he/she buys for resale to institutions that intend to either resell the goods as they are or process them in some way for resale.

Microenterprise-A term applied to extremely small service and retail businesses.

Microloans-Loans that are typically for $50,000 or less that are provided by government agencies and banks to help support very small businesses, sometimes referred to as "microentreprises." Microloans are being fostered by some federal and state policymakers as a tool for helping welfare recipients become self-supporting.

Mission Statement-A brief written acknowledgement of a company's primary purpose, values and strategies.

Money Sources-Methods of obtaining capital available to the entrepreneur. These sources include among others: family, friends, banks, private placements, factors, venture capitalists, and investment bankers.

Monopoly-A firm that holds an overwhelming degree of the market offering a specific commodity. It allows the company to exert control over prices and limit competition.

Moonlighting-Holding two jobs at the same time. Usually a part-time job is taken to supplement the income received from a regular, full-time job.

Negotiation-The bargaining, discussion and compromise between two parties in an effort to reach a settlement. In business, for example, negotiations may occur between a union representative and management to arrive at labor issues acceptable to both sides.

Net-The amount that remains after all charges and deductions are subtracted from the gross amount.

Net Income-The formula for determining net income is calculated by subtracting all expenses and taxes from total revenue. Dividends are paid out of a corporation's net income.

Net Profit-The amount of revenue that is available after all costs and expenses have been paid. However, if expenses exceed revenue, a net loss occurs.

Net Sales-The dollar amount of sales made during a specific time period, excluding sales tax and any returns or allowances.

Net Worth-The actual dollar value of the total owner's investment in your business plus any net profits that have been retained in the business from year to year determined on the balance sheet by subtracting liabilities from assets.

Network-The common channels established with important people in a variety of related fields to provide information and contacts that can be used to help the entrepreneur become successful.

New Venture-A new business providing products/services to a particular market.

Niche-A small segment of a market in which an entrepreneur feels strongly competitive.

Noncompete/Nondisclosure Agreement-Legal agreement(s) stipulating that the signee not disclose confidential information about the company and/or product, and/or preventing the signee from joining or starting a similar venture.

Not-For-Profit Corporation-An organization formed to provide to provide activities and services for society. The main focus is not on making a profit.

Note-An instrument signed by the maker (borrower) promising to pay another (the payee) a sum of money on demand or at a stated date.

Note Payable-A written promise to pay a stated sum on or by a specific date. Notes can be classified in two categories. (1) Short-term notes are due in one year or less and (2) long-term notes extend for longer periods of time.

OEM (Original Equipment Manufacturer)-A company that assembles all the necessary parts to produce a finished product.

One-Time Expense-A business expense that is not expected to recur.

Operating Budget-A financial plan outlining how a company will use its resources over a specified period of time.

Operating Expenses-The cost, including selling, administrative, and general overhead costs involved in a business's operations throughout a given time period.

Operations Manual-Typically a guide to key methods and approaches for the ongoing operations of a smaller company; it may include specifics about production, quality control, shipping, and accounting, among other areas.

Opportunity Cost-The amount of income forfeited by selecting one opportunity over another.

Organization Chart-A diagram outlining the "chain of command" that makes up the structure of a business, showing specific areas of responsibility.

Out Of Pocket Expense-Expenses incurred by an individual on a business trip that are paid for from the employee's personal funds.

Out Of Stock-A situation in which the item a customer is requesting is not currently available.

Outsourcing-The purchase of parts and equipment from outside sources.

Overdraft-A check drawn for a larger amount than the drawee has on deposit.

Overdue-A situation in which a bill is not paid or an item is not returned when due.

Overhead-Operating cost not directly associated with the product or it's marketing, such as rent, managers' salaries, administrative expenses, etc.

Partnership-A business association of two or more people. Two types of partnerships are general and limited.

Patent-A federal governmental grant to an inventor, giving exclusive rights to an invention or process for 18 years. A U.S. patent does not grant rights in foreign countries.

Payroll-An employer's list of all the employees who have earned wages or salaries over a certain period of time and the amount due to each one. Amounts are withheld from paychecks for taxes, insurance and other required and elected deductions and these withholdings are itemized on a stub that is usually attached to the paycheck.

Payroll Deductions-Sums withheld from an employee's gross pay to cover required and elected obligations. These include but are not limited to federal and state income taxes, social security, insurance premiums, contributions to pension funds and retirement plans, and so on.

Penetration Pricing-A strategy in which the price is set low in order to penetrate the market quickly.

Perpetual Inventory-A book inventory system of accounting that maintains records that continually update and disclose that amount and composition of the inventory on hand.

Personal Financial Statements-Personal balance sheets and tax returns for three years. (Sometimes required by prospective investors and loan officers of the founders/managers of the start-up.)

Physical Inventory-An itemized listing of the merchandise on hand.

Point-Of-Purchase-Advertising material placed in a high traffic area, such as a checkout register.

Popcorn Head-A person with many ideas, many of them good, who does nothing about them. He/she is in love with ideas and believes there is great virtue in large flow of them.

Pre-Tax Profit-A misconception. Profit is profit only after all expenses are deducted, and taxes are expense, a cost of doing business.

Price-The sum of money (or equivalent) for which something is bought or sold. While tradition held that it was the amount paid by the buyer, the government now leans toward the view that it is the amount received by the seller at his/her plant, the price paid by the buyer minus transportation cost.

Price Cutting-Reducing the price of products or services below the level recognized as standard and appropriate by buyers and sellers. This action is undertaken to reduce competition and hopefully lead to increased sales.

Price Discrimination-The practice of charging different prices to different buyers for goods of like grade, quality and quantity.

Price Fixing-A situation in which competitive businesses agree to establish equal prices for products and services or agree to make price changes at the same time.

Price Leader-A firm whose pricing behavior is followed by other companies in the same industry; a product/service whose price has been reduced to attract people to purchase.

Pricing Strategies-Various methods sellers of goods and services use to establish prices. (1) Retailers and wholesalers normally add a fixed percentage to their costs-called mark-up or mark-on pricing. (2) Sellers of foodstuffs and raw materials are more apt to have their prices set for them by rapidly shifting changes in external supply and demand-auction market pricing. (3) Sellers of premium goods sometimes improve demand for their goods by intentionally increasing the price-to create an aura of exclusivity around their product.

Principal-The original amount borrowed or financed; interest is paid on the principal. The face amount of a note.

Pro Forma-Indicates a projection in the future used with financial-documents list, such as pro forma Cash Flow, pro forma Income Statement, and pro forma Balance Sheet.

Product-The goods and services that consumers are able to purchase.

Product Development-The complete process of defining the functions, features, and benefits of a product or service; performing research and development from both technical and market perspectives; written plans and specifications; and building and testing prototypes and models. This process is equally relevant for both products and services.

Product Driven-An enterprise developed to exploit a new product/service. It is a product/service looking for a market.

Product Liability-The responsibility of the manufacturer, wholesaler, or retailer for damages occurring through use of the product.

Product Line-The assortment of goods marketed by a company; a group of products that are closely related because they either satisfy a class of need, are used together, are sold to the same customer groups, are marketed through the same type of outlets, or fall within given ranges.

Product Mix-The variety of products that a company offers to the public.

Product Obsolescence-A diminishing of a products' usefulness and attraction usually due to the introduction of new and improved items that perform better, are less expensive or both.

Product/Service Mix-The composite of products offered for sale by a firm or a business unit.

Production-The smooth, continuous flow of raw goods to finished goods.

Productivity-A measure of efficiency, sometimes expressed as a ratio of output to input.

Product-Life Cycle-The stages of market acceptance a product/service travels from its birth to death.

Profit-What results from revenues when all expenses have been paid.

Profit Margin-A measure of profitability; the percentage of each dollar of sales that is net income; net income divided by sales.

Profit Potential-The amount of money that can be made from a venture.

Profit Sharing-An incentive program in which a portion of the company's profits are distributed to all eligible employees.

Promotion-Efforts aimed at stimulating the demand for a product. These efforts include advertising, personal selling, publicity and special promotional events designed to gain the public's attention and interest in the seller's proposition.

Proprietary-That which is owned, such as a patent, formula, brand name, or trademark associated with the product/service.

Proprietorship-One of the simplest forms of business. An individual is the owner of the business and has full responsibility for its operation and is entitled to all profits as well as liabilities and losses.

Prospect-A potential customer who has the means to purchase a product or service, but has not made the decision to do so.

Prototype-An original model or working example of the product or innovation.

Psychographics-Analysis of consumers' psychological characteristics.

Public Accounting-The field of accounting that offers services in auditing, taxation, and management advising to the public for a fee.

Public Company-A company whose shares are sold to the public at large in accordance with Securities and Exchange Commission (SEC) regulations.

Public Offering-The sale of a company's shares of stock to the public by the company or its major stockholders.

Public Relations (PR)-Communication geared to increase public awareness and acceptance of a company, person, product or idea.

Publicity-The use of media sources to present news stories about a specific product or service.

Publicly Held Corporation-A corporation registered with the Securities and Exchange Commission (SEC); its securities are traded publicly.

Purchase Order-Formal specification sheet issued by the buyer to the supplier to secure goods or services.

Purchase Price-The amount a consumer has paid for an item.

Quality Control-The attempt to establish and maintain qualitative factors to ensure that a quality product is consistently produced. In a service industry, measures are put in place to assure that standards of performance are achieved.

Quantity Discount-A reduction in price allowed for buying certain quantities.

Quarterly Report-A report published every three months containing financial information about a company.

Questionnaire-A set of questions administered to individuals to obtain statistically useful information or to obtain feedback about personal opinion on a given subject.

Quick Assets-The sum of marketable securities, receivables and cash. Quick assets are also defined as current assets minus inventory.

Quick Ratio-The measure of a firm's liquidity or its ability to pay off liabilities quickly with the funds that are currently available. This ratio is calculated by taking the quick assets (current assets-inventory) divided by current liabilities. This ratio is also referred to as the acid-test item.

Random Sample-A limited number of observations chosen by chance from a large number of possible selections. In this form of sampling, every item in the sampling field has the same chance of being chosen as any other item.

Rate Of Return-The percentage of income earned on an investment stated as an annual figure. There are many different varieties of rate of return figures, depending on the type, purpose and maturity of the investment.

Raw Material-The unprocessed materials used to produce an item. The production process results in a change of form from the original materials.

Rebate-Usually a monetary payment made to the consumer after they have purchased an item for the full purchase price. Many rebates need to be mailed in with proof-of-purchase in order to receive the payment.

Recall- (1) An attempt to have a distributed product deemed as defective returned to the dealer or manufacturer for updating, repair, or replacement. (2) A request for employees previously laid-off to return to work.

Recruiting-An activity the personnel department engages in to seek out qualified candidates to fill openings within a company.

Remanufacturing-Manufacturing an old, worn-out product into a new and useable product.

Retailer-Any company or individual that sells commodities or goods to the ultimate consumer.

Retained Earnings-Net income that is kept within the organization.

Retainer-A fee given to an attorney in exchange for his advice or services or a claim on his services if a future need for them occurs.

Return On Assets (ROA)-Measures a company's ability to produce net profits by effectively utilizing its assets. The higher the ratio, the more effective the company is at using its assets to produce profits.

Return On Equity (ROE)-Measures the return on the owner's investment in the company and is perhaps the most important measure of a business' financial viability. The higher the ratio, the higher the rate of return on the owner's investment.

Return On Sales (ROS)-**Measures the percent of every dollar in sales that a company maintains as net profit after all direct and indirect expenses are paid. The higher the ratio, the more profits being captured from each dollar of sales.**

Return To Vendor (RTV)-Merchandise that is returned to the vendor by the receiving store. A few of the reasons the items might be returned are wrong style(s) were shipped, merchandise was received late or damaged in shipment, etc.

Revenue-The gross income received before any expenses are deducted.

Reverse Marketing-A method that reverses traditional marketing procedures by focusing on current and qualified prospects and using techniques that induce customers to come to the seller.

ROI (Return On Investment)-The amount earned in proportion to the capital invested, usually stated as a percentage.

S Corporation (Sub-Chapter S Corporation)-A firm that has elected to be taxed as a partnership under the sub-chapter S provision of the Internal Revenue Code.

Sales Budget-Detailed projection of sales by product for a future period of time; the sales expense projected; anticipated cost of the sales operation.

Sales Cycle-The average period of time it takes for the sales organization to close on a sale-from the initial contact with a prospective customer to writing up the order. Different products and services have widely varying sales cycles, with more complex and expensive products usually having longer cycles.

Sales Forecast-A projection of the anticipated sales volume of a product or service.

Sales Manager-A person who oversees the planning and directing of sales efforts in his designated area of responsibilities. In addition, this person usually supervises one or more sales people.

Sales Pitch-A statement directed at potential customers to entice them to purchase a product or service.

Sales Plan-Setting specific goals, volume in dollars and/or units, and the strategy anticipated to accomplish them.

Sales Potential-The ratio of a venture's sales to the total industry sales of the available market.

Sales Quota-A sales goal assigned to a marketing unit for use in the management of its sales efforts.

Sales Rep-Abbreviation for sales representative. A salesperson.

SBA (Small Business Administration)-Federal agency created in 1953 that assists with business loans and other problems relating to the operation of small business.

SBA Backed Loan-Obtained from banking sources, an SBA loan provides guarantee for a percentage of a loan.

Search Engines-Programs such as Yahoo, Lycos, and Infoseek that let you search the distributed database of the World Wide Web.

Seasonality-Variation of sales activity caused by the time of the year.

Seed Capital-Money used by the entrepreneur in the beginning stages of an enterprise.

Seed Stage-An investment strategy involving portfolio companies that have not yet fully established commercial operations, and may also involve continued operations, and may also involve continued research and product development.

Self-Employed-Describes an individual who earns income from a business which he/she owns rather than receives a salary or wage from an employer.

Self-Service-A retail establishment in which customers serve themselves and complete the transaction by paying the cashier.

Service-An intangible function that benefits the consumer.

Service Mark-A word or symbol used by a service organization, similar to a trademark for a product or product company. Protection is covered by the U.S. Patent and Trademark Office.

Shelf Life-The length of time a product continues to be saleable or aesthetically pleasant to customers.

Short-Term Debt-Loans that are to be repaid within one year.

SIC Codes (Standard Industry Codes)-A system established by the United States Government for categorizing various businesses according to their specific industry, with a unique code belonging to each industrial category.

Silent Investor-A financial partner in an organization who is not officially or publicly recognized as an equity stakeholder in the venture.

Silent Partner-A partner who has a financial interest in the company but plays no active role, even though he/she may be known to the public as a partner.

Small Business Investment Company (SBIC)-A program of the Small Business Administration (SBA), Small Business Investment Companies are licensed investment firms that use private capital along with SBA backed debentures to help finance small businesses. For more information go to: http://www.sba.gov/INV/howtoseeks.html

Social Entrepreneur-Someone who uses the methods of business entrepreneurs to achieve social goals, such as creating new jobs or helping disadvantaged communities.

Soft Sell-A sales technique that uses a low-pressured approach.

Sole Proprietorship-A business firm owned by only one person and operated for his/her profit.

Special Order- (1) A customer's request forwarded to a vendor ordering an item that is not carried in stock or is temporarily out of stock. (2) An order submitted by a retailer requesting specially manufactured merchandise to supplement the store's present product mix. The merchandise requested is not in the vendor's regular stock.

Specialty Goods-Consumer goods having unique characteristics and/or brand identification for which a significant group of buyers are habitually willing to make a special purchasing effort, such as fancy food, stereo components, sporting equipment, cameras, men's suits.

Specialty Store-Retail outlet carrying a large selection in limited merchandise lines such as women's or men's clothing.

Specialty Stores-Retail outlets that concentrate on specific classifications of merchandise and carry a large selection of items in the area of specialization. Examples include books, jewelry, furniture and shoe stores.

Spin-off-A divestiture of business operation into a separate legal entity.

Start-Up Capital-Money needed to launch a new venture during the pre-start-up and initial period of operation.

Stock Certificate-A document issued to a stockholder by a corporation indicating the number of shares of stock owned by the stockholder.

Stock Dividend-A proportional distribution of securities to the company's stockholders.

Stock Exchange-A place where the buying and selling of securities can occur in an organized setting.

Stock Purchase Plan-A plan that allows employees to buy company stock, usually at a discounted price. In some cases, the employer contributes to the purchase.

Stockholders-The owners of a corporation.

Stockholders' Equity-The portion of a business owned by the stockholders.

Straight-Line Depreciation-A method of depreciation in which capital cost is amortized in equal periodic amounts over the estimated life of an asset.

Subcontract-An arrangement that allows a third party to come in and complete all or part of the work indicated in the original contract.

Sublease-A lease made by a tenant to another person.

Suggestive Selling-A strategy of selling in which salespeople recommend additional items related to those the customer asks about and is likely to purchase or has already bought. This technique can be used to introduce newly arrived merchandise, items on sale, etc.

Takeover-The purchase of one company by another.

Tangible Assets-Assets that are touchable and real as opposed to intangible assets, which are not of a physical or material nature.

Target Customers-A store's marketing effort directed to specific people in an attempt to entice them into the store and become customers.

Target Market-The market selected for penetration by a firm's management.

Target Pricing-An attempt at pricing items to maximize both sales and profit.

Tax Benefits-The deductions, protection, savings and shelters that result from investing in a business.

Taxable Income-The amount of income left after all allowable deductions and exemptions have been subtracted. This remaining income is therefore taxable.

Telemarketing-The combination of computers and telephones to effect automated telemarketing.

Term Loan-A loan with an original maturity beyond one year.

Terms-The specifications set forth for repaying loans or paying invoices: the time limits and amount to be paid.

Test Market-The focus of a controlled study carried out in a carefully selected marketplace. The study's purpose is usually to test how successful a new marketing strategy will be before undertaking the expense of distributing it to a broader marketing base.

Testimonial-An endorsement of a product by a satisfied customer or a celebrity.

Total Assets-The actual dollar value of all tangible and intangible property owned or maintained by a company at any point in time. These are the operational resources a business maintains, such as cash, short-term investments, accounts receivable, inventory, furniture, fixtures, equipment, buildings, land, etc.

Trade Association-A not-for-profit organization that exists to support its members. Usually, those that belong to a trade association work in closely related occupations.

Trade Discount-A discount allowed to various customers on the list price of merchandise before the credit terms apply. These discounts are used to encourage prompt payment.

Trade Dress-A legal concept that embraces such proprietary retail design components as signage, color schemes, and uniforms. It also applies to Web site design features.

Trade Secret-Any type of information, including a formula, pattern, compilation, program, device, method, technique or process that derives independent value from not being generally known to other persons who can obtain economic value from its disclosure or use.

Trade Show-An industry-wide market where many manufacturers demonstrate their products and actively solicit sales.

Trademark™-A brand or part of a brand that is given legal protection because it is capable of exclusive appropriation.

Turnaround-The successful efforts to reverse the financial downfall of a company.

Turnkey Operation-A product/service concept, completely assembled, installed, or set up to begin operation which is then leased or sold to an individual to run as his/her own venture.

Turnover- (1) The number of people that are hired into an organization within a period to replace those that leave. Sometimes this figure is calculated as a ratio by taking the number of people who have joined the company as well as the number of the people who have left during a specific period of time for every 100 employees. (2) The frequency with which an asset, such as inventory, is replaced during a period of time, usually a year.

Undercapitalization-A situation in which a new enterprise starts with too little money to carry it through the beginning stages of development.

Underemployed-A situation in which a person working at a job for which he or she is over qualified.

Union-A labor organization whose major objective is to promote members' interest when negotiating with employers.

Unit Cost-The cost incurred in the production of one unit of product; usually computed by dividing total production cost by the number of units produced for a given time period.

Unlimited Liability-A legal situation in which the owner of a business is fully liable for all of its debts and obligations to the extent of his or her total estate. People who enter business with unlimited liability can be pauperized through little fault of their own.

Value Added-The process of enhancing a basic product.

Variable Cost-A cost that changes in total in direct proportion to productive output or any other volume measure.

Vendor-The source of supply, raw materials or finished goods throughout the production and distribution processes.

Venture-A business endeavor that involves a high level of risk and chance.

Venture Capital-Money from investment pools or firms that specialize in financing young companies' growth, usually in return for stock.

W-2 Form-Wage and Tax Statement. By the end of January of each year, employers must provide each employee with at least two copies of his or her withholding statement-showing earnings for the preceding year and various deductions. Employees must file one copy of their W-2 Forms with their federal income tax form.

Wage-Compensation given to an employee in exchange for work performed. Wages vary and can be paid per piece, per hour, or per day or in any other period or unit that has been previously agreed upon.

Wholesaling-All activities involved in selling goods or services to those who are buying for the purpose of resale or business use.

Word-Of-Mouth Advertising- One satisfied customer tells another about a particular product of service.

Workers' Compensation Insurance-Mandated insurance payments made by employers to cover their employees' work-related injuries and diseases.

Working Capital-The amount of funds available to pay short-term expenses. Seen as a cushion to meet unexpected or out-of-the-ordinary expenses. It is determined by subtracting current liabilities from current assets.

WWW (World Wide Web)-A vast collection of information in hypertext and hypermedia format on "home pages."